True Cold Crimes

True Crime Stories That Took Years to Crack

(True Stories of Murders That Took Years or Decades to Solve)

Miriam Hoy

Published By **Tyson Maxwell**

Miriam Hoy

True Cold Crimes: True Crime Stories That Took Years to Crack (True Stories of Murders That Took Years or Decades to Solve)

ISBN   978-1-77485-577-5

No part of this guidebook shall be reproduced in any form without permission in writing from the publisher except in the case of brief quotations embodied in critical articles or reviews.

Legal & Disclaimer

expenses, including any legal fees potentially resulting from the application of any of the information provided by this guide. This disclaimer applies to any damages or injury caused by the use and application, whether directly or indirectly, of any advice or information presented, whether for breach of contract, tort, negligence, personal injury, criminal intent, or under any other cause of action.

You agree to accept all risks of using the information presented inside this book. You need to consult a professional medical practitioner in order to ensure you are both able and healthy enough to participate in this program.

Table of contents

Chapter 1: The Mysterious Murder Of Patsy Wright

Patsy Bolton Wright was a gorgeous, vibrant as well-off woman, who appeared to have everything she wanted. She owned the world-renowned wax museum in Grand Prairie, Texas. She was a trainer and presented horses. She was a socialite and audacious woman with no enemies. In 1987, her death was shocking.

Patsy used to take an e-capsule of NyQuil to aid her in getting to sleep. However, at 3:00 am the sister called to tell her that something was not right. She was unable to breathe. Patsy was poisoned by strychnine. The substance was found within the NyQuil bottle that was beside her mattress. Even though the police initially thought she was suffering from suicide, they later ruled out the possibility. It was later discovered that Patsy Wright was not suicidal.

In reality she was preparing to embark on a new phase of investigation, and sifting through the muck of an unsettling divorce and family secrets could not uncover her killer, however. There are plausible suspects.

Prairie, Texas is just to the east from Arlington in the middle of Dallas Fort Worth and Dallas Fort worth. It was created through Alexander Mick Ray Deckmann and 1863. He was a resident of Birdville then renamed Haltom city. He discovered that it was possible to trade his wagon and oxen with property located in Dallas County. Then he purchased about 250 acres.

What is currently downtown grand Prairie is named after him. He gave Wright of right of way for TNP railroad TNP railway company in 1867. And in the summer of 1876 track extensions were made across Deckmann until Fort worth. TNP railroad created some confusion calling the trucks that traveled from Fort Worth towards Dallas in the grand prairie, due to its location at the Eastern portion of the vast prairie that extended to West Texas.

Yes, the office was founded in 1877. The confusion grew since the postmaster mispelled Dykeman and the name used for the area shown on maps was grand Prairie from the 1850s onwards. Inconsistencies in the name created problems with the delivery of mail for business and residents, especially after the Grand Prairie independently-run school district was created in 1902.

The Post Office officially changed the address for Deckmann into grand Prairie. The town was officially incorporated in 1909 and the name was altered to Grand Prairie. Downtown was full of the grocery and dry goods store as well as a cotton gin, two blacksmiths hotel in a drugstore and a lumberyard barbershop. even a stand selling short-order items that sold barbecues and cold drinks in 1929.

The Curtis Wright flying service open close to the area of Dalworth to begin Grand Prairie's rich history of aviation. The town went through the Great Depression, just like the rest of the nation. In 1931 Clyde Barrow and Ray Hamilton took over the inner city ticket offices in downtown Grand Prairie.

This would be Clyde who was Bonnie and Clyde when world war II began in 1939 The war department granted permission to the Navy to make use of Hensley field, which was rechristened The Naval reserves aviation bases. Much of the 20th century was characterized by the growth of the city. The vault facility for aircraft created a number of jobs for residents, defense and aircraft manufacturing continue to be the mainstay of the city's economy to this day.

In 1972, however, grand Prairie became famous for being the new home of the Southwestern wax museum that was a historical one. It was originally situated at Dallas the fairgrounds. The museum started its fascinating story. In the year 1870, a Clay County deputy sheriff, and two other wealthy citizens started collecting antique firearms.

The sheriff had ties with numerous Outlaws since the clay counties' northern majority border is located along the Oklahoma border. The partner Henry Harrison Schwind developed relationships with law enforcers and, as his interest became more well-known

He was able to acquire firearms from legendary law enforcement officers such as to the Texas Rangers to the U S Marshall's in 1957. in which Thomas Bolton purchased the collection of guns and was captivated by wax models of famous people after his visit to Madame Tussauds' wax museum and London where the idea of a perfect society was born.

In addition to securing loans from other investors and partners Bolton created Bolton's Southwestern Historical wax Museum in Dallas in 1963. His goal was to draw attention to the collection's uniqueness by displaying replicas of the most famous and notorious historical figures of the Old West as well as more modern texts on history. The museum made wax was an enormous success.

The owners were struggling to cope with the crowd they decided to relocate the park to a larger venue in the grand Prairie. When it opened again in 1972, there were wax figures and guns such as Poncho, Wild Bill Hickok. and Billy the child were with them were recreations of famous scenes such as the assassination of JFK and Dallas.

Warren Beatty donated the car used in the film Bonnie and Clyde to the exhibit at the museum , as well as wax models from Beatty along with Faye Dunaway. When the exhibit of Bonnie was also raised the museum attracted more than 250,000 visitors per year. The museum was not long after it relocated to Grand Prairie. Tom Bolton's daughters Sally Horning and Patricia Bolton became co-owners. By the time they were co-owners, it was worth around a million dollars by the time it was.

The sole siblings born to Tom Bolton and Virginia Bolton, Sally and Patsy Bolton were raised in the city parks, where they attended Hillcrest high school. Virginia was a typical housewife. Tom was an oilman wealthy and had an uncanny love of Texas the past. In the beginning of the seventies Bolton, the late Mr. Bolton and his new wife and daughter, Sally and Patsy, all relocated to the Arlington region.

Sally was a student at Texas Tech for two years, and later took business school classes. Patsy was known as to be a head Turner and a luminous blonde with a beautiful passion for life. As accomplished as she was an executive but her true passion was horses. She along with Sally performed admirably managing the museum.

There was a bit of sibling rivalry and jealousy. Patsy was pretty and attractive, and males were swarming around her like fly-like insects. She was an Dallas socialite who attended charity events, galas, parties and opening evenings. She could be found at every social gathering. She was a fan of driving around town in the Red Porsche as well as her Lincoln towncar.

Following college Patsy got married by a gentleman by the name of bill, Wright. In the month of January was 1965, seven years later, the couple and sister assumed the museum. Bill had been an executive with a department store chain and, unsurprisingly, a loner. The couple resided in Arlington and had a good time there for a time. They had two children,

Leslie and Wayne, and they were content for a long time.

In the year that Tom Bolton died in 1976 The sisters were fighting in court over their inheritance. Together with their stepmother. Patsy and Sally were successful in winning the case and became the owners of their father's prestigious museum. However, the tense court case was a lesson for Patsy the lesson. She pledged that her children would not have to fight for what was legally theirs. Patsy and Bill divorced in the month of October, 1980.

And it was very friendly. She was given the house along with the ranch as well as three saddle horses. She received the Cadillac which was an 18 foot boat. Along with the majority of the house furniture was moved to Houston and then remarried. However, when he died in 2005 his body was laid to rest with Patsy. Then, to her family's delight, they learned that she was the executor named by her estate.

In the month of January, the year 1981 Patsy was introduced to a person known as Bob Cox when he called the museum asking her and Sally whether they would be interested in purchasing his wax museum which included all American presidents. Cox was a professional poker player, and also was the owner of his rival museum along together with his wife, Kitty, Bob Cox wanted out from the museum business and out of his union with his wife.

They and Katie were divorced. Even though talks regarding the purchase of the Museum failed over, he insists for her advice to call her once the divorce was over. He did, and they began to date a few months later, with Patsy believing. He was then single. His age was 14. younger than her and had his own glamorous group of friends and also a country club. He was treated Patsy as a queen.

However, when she discovered that he was still married, she forced to have him divorced from his wife. They visited Galveston in the beginning of January in 1983, where Cox planned to create the creation of a wax museum next to the Sea Wall. Already, there were set-up figures, costumes as well as other materials for the museum, but it was lying in an abandoned structure.

Cox had a plan to remodel and renovate the building, aiming to open it to the peak tourist season. However, on February 1 the building was caught in fire and destroyed the majority of the museum's collection. The next day, Bob and kitty Cox had their divorce finalized. In March of 1983 Bob along with Patsy got married in Dallas in the year 1983. C would later inform friends and relatives that on the day the wedding day of Bob Cox had changed.

He wasn't his charming man. She realized. Then he began verbally abusing towards her and her kids even though. Bob was adamant to reside at Arlington along with Patsy until her children completed high school. He was unhappy, which made the situation even more difficult. Bob did not contribute to the marital finances in any way. Patsy took care of everything.

The house The utilities, the groceries. Then she realized that he would spend his entire afternoon playing at the Dallas country club, playing poker. Patsy was aware that he was gambler, but did not realize what the problem was. Kenny Cox cited his gambling addiction in her divorce application, frightened that his addiction would cause financial hardship for the family.

The real end of Patsy's marriage to Bob Cox was when the IRS called her. They wanted to tie the earnings of her husband to his tax liabilities totaling around $300,000. It was smart of her to sign a prenuptial contract. However, she later revealed to her friends that Cox attempted to Sue to stay clear of kitty. Cox was able to describe her former husband as a stepping stone to Patsy and advising her to leave the marriage as quickly as she was able to.

Bob left just a day before their anniversary. A week later, Patsy declared divorce on April 1984. However, Bob tried everything to stay out of being served. The papers were in effect for two months. A month later, Patsy requested an order of restraining, claiming she was concerned that Bob was stalking and harassing her.

He said it was due to the fear that she'd be denied the country club's membership after divorce, which is absurd. Patsy did not have a desire for joining the club. She was in good social standing within her own. Right. She was just looking to get out of the marriage, with her assets in tact. The friends of Patsy's later stated they believed that Bob Cox had started following her around, parking in front of her home at night and was even dressed in disguises such as Sally and had a divorce and then was remarried to Steve Horning in 1981.

There was clearly tension between her sister Patsy and her husband. Sally had been introduced to Steve during the time his landscaping business worked on a project to the Museum. Steve was a few years older than Sally however to her friends it was an obvious love-match. Patsy was at first happy for her sister, however, her perception of Steve was quickly changed.

Friends of hers later said that Patsy said that she considered Steve the phony, and that she hated Steve. Steve was a dreamer of becoming a rancher and also playing the big game. Hunter and Patsy were shocked when, only a few years after the Horning wedding, she found that her brother-in-law's money had been used up all the inheritance Sally received. Then, in June 1987 she took steps to ensure Steve Horning would never end having any of her property.

The sisters had initially had a plan to have a buy sell agreement. Each of them had $500,000 in Life insurance. If one person died one of the sisters could buy her stock shares in the museum. In this way, one Bolton sister would be the sole stockholder. The agreement was signed in the month of June in 1985. However, over the next two years that followed, certain things had occurred which made Patsy uncomfortable about the agreement.

The museum's value was up significantly and the sisters had purchased a museum located in San Antonio and we're planning the Ripley's Believe it or not collection of unusual and interesting objects. In autumn of 1985 Sally became ill with cancer. She along with Steve had been experiencing issues with their marriage prior to being diagnosed, however Steve was extremely supportive of his wife throughout her disease.

Patsy was aware the fact that two grandparents had died from cancer, and that Sally's outlook was not very good. If Sally passed away in the first place, with the buy-sell contract in force, Steve would inherit half one million dollars. Although she was impressed by Steve's care for his sister Patsy did not trust Steve, Sally was treated with chemotherapy.

In the end of summer 1986, she was fully remission and was in full remission, however she agreed with Patsy that their initial agreement needed to be revised. The sisters set up a board meeting for early November to review the new agreement.

A few months prior to Patsy Wright's passing on the cutting horse race in the Mesquite rodeo She was also planning to buy a ranch of 30 acres in the town of Ledo in which she could keep the horse she named Dry Leo along with another 3-year old golding. She was the owner, but she had already sold the house. She lived her home with Bob Cox about three months prior to this , and was renting a home until she was able to move back to her ranch.

On the Thursday morning of the 22nd of October in 1987 her job was with a trainer for horses. Her goal was to take on dry Leo and compete in more races. It was a feat of courage and athleticism however, Patsy believed she could handle the challenge of her inheritance and the money she earned from the Museum. Patsy became a billionaire and, while living the life of a socialite but her ultimate goal was to have horses to exhibit and be a competitor.

She paid $26,000 for dry Leo and was ecstatic for him the next morning. She put $1500 down on the Mayer. She had a plan to breed. Her dream was coming true. She was soon to live in the countryside with her horses and continue her job in the museums. A number of friends were worried about her being a single woman in a rural setting, but she brushed aside concerns.

She did however purchase an Glock automated pistol. She was very busy renovating her home and building her stable. On the evening of the 22nd of October, Patsy hosted a cocktail event to launch the Halloween tours of 1987 at the museum. There were wax models and actors in scary costumes. It was a dress rehearsal , and she thought it was to be the most important event in the calendar.

The dress rehearsal dinner was a huge success , and Patsy returned home exhausted and happy. When she returned home, she was around 9 pm and called several times. Her son Wayne Wright later said when they spoke to her she sounded good. Actually, she was amazing. She had made herself eggs scrambled, and changed into her pajamas , before she lay down in her King size bed of water.

But sleep didn't come. It was likely that she was still pumped up from the celebration. Therefore, she took a dose of NyQuil. She frequently took one capful of the drug to aid in her sleep. It was even it was known to her family and friends. It was discovered to be helpful when her babies were still teething, and began taking it regularly her own. Patsy considered it to be the cure for everything, and one of her friends made fun of her for being an NyQuil head.

At 3:00 AM, Patsy telephoned her younger sister Sally. Sally told her in a whispered voice, I've had an amount of NyQuil and there's something very wrong. I'm experiencing breathing problems. Sally phoned the police but couldn't find the address of her rental home. Then she along with Steve took their cars and drove over to the house.

It was only one mile away. It was not locked at the front, and Sally thought of the time that Patsy told her that her spare key was recently been lost. Steve was at the back of the house and climbed inside the bedroom windows that were wide open to enjoy cooling breeze. Steve stated that it appeared like she had been thrown off on the mattress.

He rushed and allowed Sally inside the front door. They observed that the alarm system for Patsy wasn't set. The system was set. It was put in place after she noticed many windows broken, and with a restraining order against her. In mind was her ex-husband. There was nothing stolen, however. There were many valuable items in her home however, it made her feel uncomfortable.

However, for reasons unknown the alarm wasn't set for that particular night. Steven Sally said that Patsy's eyes were opened but they were not focused. They tried to wake her to open her eyes, but they couldn't call the number nine-one, one and then soon. Paramedics and firefighters arrived afterward. A paramedic at the scene told it was already late. Patsy had no pulse, no blood pressure.

Her eyes were beginning to shrink however, they were able to transport her into an ambulance and took her into Arlington Memorial hospital. It's 4:15 am. The official declaration of her death was made. The ER doctor did not know what had happened to Patsy and an autopsy was carried out by the Tarrant County medical examiner, however, they did not find anything that was obvious to suggest that she had died. apparently healthy, active 43-year-old woman.

Steve was reported to police that he attempted to perform CPR on her sister-in-law , and that when he put a blow into her mouth, green fluid would enter his mouth and he would then spit it out. Although the crime wasn't being investigated at the moment, a quick-thinking policeman seized the bottle of NyQuil and placed it in an evidence bag while her family members cried and set up funeral arrangements.

Her daughter Leslie received a mysterious phone call one day after her mother's passing. She claimed that the phone caller wanted to talk with her mom. When she informed her her mother passed away, to the grave, the woman stated, "Good. I was hoping she would die. She was thinking at the time that it was an innocent prank, but it would turn out to be more insidious.

Sergeant Jake Gustafson of the Arlington police department was assigned to the case on Monday morning. just three days following

Patsy Wright's passing. His supervisor put the folder over his desk and told him, Gus, there's something wrong here. Gustafson was an untrained homicide detective who knew inside his head.

After he had was able to read the report in its entirety, he realized the report was suspicious of death. There was not a suicide note, there was no drugs, not even NyQuil, which is a prescription drug. NyQuil and to a healthy woman aged 43. was not simply dead with no obvious cause. There was no indication for forced entry. Steve Horning had told police that he moved a table that had two plates in order in order to get to Patsy.

If he attempted CPR the information was not logical, particularly considering the conversation Patsy had about her child. Patsy was very specific about being at home and cooking herself some eggs before going to bed, but Gustafson believed his gut instinct and sent Patsy's tissues and blood samples off to be tested. The Tarrant County Medical Examiner contacted him, he inquired whether he was sitting down. the poison was strychnine, he replied that it was, and the poison wouldn't be detected on a standard toxicology panel conducted by Emmy Gustafson.

Remember the NyQuil bottle, which was found in the lab and then had it examined. The test was positive and confirmed to restriction nine, it actually included eight times the amount that normally kills the human body. Strychnine is often referred to as the poison of the lover, however this is an inaccurate name. It's an extremely horrific and painful method of dying.

Your muscles begin to twitch. You feel like you. Before you take over your feet and head, move forward. Your face is blue as the mouth turns into a disgusting grin with every violent twitch. There is a long period of waiting. The anticipation of a new one. The fear and feeling of helplessness will be frightening following three to four seizures.

The death of the patient will be accompanied through paralysis of the breathing muscles as well as Patsy Wright. Was killed by an undiluted version that of the poison. A form of the poison is approximately 3 percent. Strychnine is employed to kill rats in gophers. Other pests in Patsy's Dos could only be purchased legally from chemical manufacturers who sell it to approved buyers.

This is the reason why, as poison that strychnine is seldom used in murders. Just a few days after it was discovered Gustafson along with a group of experts, which included the FBI as well as a representative from the VIX corporation, which makes NyQuil had a meeting. The poisoning incident was the only one that were linked to the lot number that was on the Patsy's NyQuil bottle.

The moment the FBI released a report on products tampering, the matter was reopened in Gustafson in the form of an incidental case that was not homicide an Emmy from Tarrant County Emmy ruled her death was not a suicide because suicide or the possibility of homicide being totally eliminated. However, family and friends have maintained that Patsy Wright wouldn't be a suicide victim.

The museum's director stated, quote: Patsy wouldn't let her life go. She was passionate about life. Her personality was extroverted, joyful and self-sufficient. She could sweep anyone off their feet with her enthusiasm. Her children , too, strongly denied. This was suicide. Leslie Wright said, quote that there's no way to believe this was suicide. She was living her life to the fullest. for.

She was a successful businesswoman and lived a comfortable life. She competed in the races on her horses. She was extremely content. The family does not feel as though she would have committed suicide. She was a highly positive person, especially given the pain of her death could be. Patsy endured, and the investigators were in agreement however they needed to demonstrate that.

The Tarrant County medical examiner has ordered an autopsy on the psychological condition on Patsy Wright. The psychologist spoke with Patsy's friends and family to assess her mental state. In the year of her passing away, the physician determined that Patsy had a low-risk for suicide. She was not under financial pressure. She was in good health condition and was thinking about her future.

Even set her alarm clock set to the following morning. She didn't meet any of the guidelines for suicide. This proved everything. Detective Gustafson believed in. He believed that the killing was personal strychnine that was an painful death. It seemed like revenge to him, particularly considering the massive dose contained in the bottle, enough to kill up to nine or eight people.

He began looking at the motives and opportunities. He stated, quote, that money can be a motivator. As for revenge, love and hate, sometimes it's anger or retaliation. Who gains from her death, but is at risk if she won't die. And for the perpetrator to be able to be able to be aware of the NyQuil habit.

All of this pointed to someone. There was a person who was near to the investigators who. They started looking into things and even her private life was not in line with her happy appearance. Patsy's family revealed public tension and an odd relationship with her husband for instance. Gustafson said that this wasn't necessarily a crime that required urgent nature.

If the perpetrator knew about her habits, he/she would have just wait till she required the tiny glass of NyQuil to ease her sleep. Perhaps they were aware of her busy schedule during the day, but maybe the plan was put in place earlier. However, he was also convinced it was possible that they had other indications to indicate that she was not in a room by herself that night. All light bulbs were turned on, and the television was on.

If seed Horning is to be believed the reports, two plates were in her bed. It's possible. The only thing is that she didn't mention the late-night guest to her son while they talked. Someone surprised Gustafson by naming him a suspect. Steve Horny and Sally were arguing with Patsy's adult children over their inheritance. Leslie and Wainwright were urging to get the Hornings to respect the new contract which Patsy and Sally had planned to draft.

They would rather have their mother stock than the cash Sally was refusing to pay. Then they told them they were young, in addition, pointing out it was far higher than at the time that the original agreement was concluded. This is quite strange to me. The dynamics of the family are often a bit bizarre, and certainly not the first family to argue over an inheritance of a significant amount for the part of his son.

Steven sister, Steve and Sally were drafting quotes, wills with a solid foundation that would grant them the museums at the time of our deaths. However, if Sally passed away before Steve had died, he would be the owner of a majority stake in the museum. This was exactly what Patsy tried to stop as the investigation went nowhere The situation was about to get more bizarre eleven months after Patsy's demise.

On September 9 1988, the grand Prairie wax museum burned by a fire. The initial theory was that it could be the result of an electric short. The museum's 39,000 square feet as well as the more than 300 wax models as well as priceless antiques and artifacts were completely destroyed. The estimated damage to be in the region of $8 million. There was speculation about the fact that the fire had been planned to erase evidence of the murder of Patsy in the museum.

The electrical box that was faulty was blamed initially for the fire. Marshall insists that it was an arson. Within a few minutes, the entire building was destroyed. This is not something that happens. Yet the investigation was halted after the initial case file was stolen from a locked area at the Grand Prairie fire department. As the Marshall was scrambling to put an inquest into place. were thefts arising from the wreckage.

Sorting through Ash and other debris. The gun was able to make an appearance with the huge gun collection. They wouldn't have been ignited or burned as easily as the other guns. Yeah. Today the descendants of the first proprietor of these firearms Henry Harrison, Schwind continue to look for the guns they took care of about 100 of the 300 missing.

Arson investigators believed a lot of this. They were simply searching for souvenirs. There was one arrest made just two weeks after the fire. A 23-year-old mortuary student known as Stanley Lester pointer was arrested for removing an object from the rebel. However, the Dallas grand jury lowered the charges to criminal violation of the law.

The former museum was cleared and 18 months after, the wax museum in the Southwest opened as the palace. The story-building was decorated with lavender, pink and gold and infused with Arabian influences. It was a Ripley's Believe it or is not. Exhibit included. Sally Horning was well aware of the rumors within the community of Patsy's murder and the fire, as well as the mystery surrounding the murder, and the fire did nothing but to increase revenue for the new museum.

So , she and Steve employed an attorney to act as a legal advisor to assist in the investigation into the death of Patsy. Her ex-husband, bill Wright had been surprised to meet her family members to find out. He was her executor estate. He was questioned, had a polygraph test and was cleared. He then joined his two children Leslie and Wayne and hired an private investigator to investigate on the case.

Yes, I William deer, came aboard. He claimed to be an'modern' James Bond solving cases, the police that you've let go on this journalist. I thought of him as the ambulance hunter. He would often get himself in cases with a high profile. To be fair the book he wrote was known as OJ is innocent and I'm able to prove it.

I believe his shady fame was earned. The fire detective Gustafson was notified of another woman mysteriously dying working at the museum in the beginning of the eighties. Laurie Ann Williams was head secretary when, in September 1984, she was dismissed from work suffering extreme abdominal discomfort. A procedure was carried out to remove her appendix however, doctors were puzzled when they discovered the organ to be healthy.

And Lori kept getting worse and was dying. 11 days after her death. The death was officially determined due to pneumonia caused by viral infection. As a result of the surgery, Gustafson asked for the medical examiner to examine the files of Lori, but could not find evidence that matched strychnine poisoning. However, family members who were already worried now needed answers.

They raised the necessary $750 to exhume her body. It was more than two years since the death of Patsy Wright. Private investigator Bill Deer collected soil samples near the grave of Lori to ensure there was no doubt of pesticides or herbicides being the cause of any poisons that could be detected in Laurie's body. The autopsy, however, revealed there was no evidence of poison.

Bill Deere pointed out that the poison might have been metabolized prior to her death, but there was no proof that Laurie was killed. Still. He claims that Patsy discovered something she didn't want to have seen in the museum. He stated, quote: I believe Lori

Williams was murdered to make it difficult for Patsy Wright.

The police chief was even to be in agreement that the museum's wax was a common thread in all of the areas of investigation were covered. He also spoke of drug trafficking, gunrunning as well as the smuggling and trafficking of illegal aliens However, I would like you to look at Patsy's past. She was a successful businesswoman managing shares in an extremely profitable business.

Her father built. She was just buying the ranch and was obsessed in acquiring horses and preparing horses for competition. This may sound like naivety but I don't believe she was involved in any illegal activity. There was no need for it. She was already wealthy and the ghost of the bill Deere created of her stumble into illegal activities at the museum, kept her in the rumors about the fire and her death.

Soon, family and friends began pointing fingers at one others. And even Leslie as well as Wain Wright who were her children who were both students at Texas tech , were investigated and polygraphed. They were able to inherit some money however they were cleared of the matter right away. Patsy did have a boyfriend at the time who was named Larry Todd, but he was a cover for his own.

It was one of the calls she made on the night that she died. He was in Austin and according to reports the man was devastated by the murder investigation. They then zeroed on the couple that were in the process of boarding Patsy's horses. While she waited for her ride, she was able to pay towards the ranch, Bonnie Alexander had cashed a check of $4,000.

Patsy wrote the note on the day prior to her death. Experts in handwriting discovered that although Patsy had written the word saddle on her notes she didn't actually written in the total amount. A couple of Alexanders did that , and added the word fees after that and the saddle. On the day of her death she had contacted her accountant and requested him to liquidate some of her assets so that she could get $125,000 in cashthat she needed to complete closing the Elaina ranch which she had moved by two weeks.

The accountant specifically asked whether there were any other outstanding large checks to be paid. And Patsy did not have any, probably 4,000 was not a huge amount to Patsy however, it seemed suspicious to investigators as well as her accountant. Then it was revealed that Patsy was a bit expensive. Horses were in fact still under Alexander's name.

The Alexanders had given her the keys to the Alexanders and paid for their boarding. She was even spending the month of June in their home until they discovered her house rental. However, Bonnie Alexander explained to police that Patsy just gave them a check and instructed that they should add up the amount she owed for several months of boarding as well as the entry fee to contests.

Bonnie also explained why the horses were in the husband's and wife's names. Patsy was afraid of her brother-in law to have access to the horses. If anything were to happen in her life, Steve Horning had already been a suspect to the police, and there was definitely family drama going on. The sister and her mother were scheduled to hold an appointment in the two weeks following her death to discuss a new financial arrangement.

Dear PR bill I thought the Alexanders could have had a different reason for jealousy. The bill may have was rejected by Patsy. In turn, Bonnie might've been jealous of her. Perhaps they were poisoned? Patsy bill Deere discovered that strychnine is sometimes utilized by breeders of horses in small amounts to treat their horses.

He requested Alexander Alexanders to complete polygraph exams and they were able to pass. It's an intriguing theory. The check business seems suspicious, but it's also likely that they were Patsy's buddies. She was living with him for a whole month. She stayed with her horses at the stables. She was trained by bill Alexander.

It's quite possible. They did receive an unsigned check. This amount of money would not be a huge loss to her bank account. If her accounting professional was not aware of the fact that it was there. And , naturally, even with Steve being as a suspect Sally as well as Steve Horning were definitely on Detective Gustafson's radar and the paramedics and police of bill deer. were not aware of the table. Steve claimed that he had removed the table he been held in the table.

They also doubted his claim that liquid was leaking from Patsy's mouth. A paramedic at the scene, stated that there was no success in performing CPR on the woman. So, even if he had tried mouth-to-mouth but the attempt was not successful. The woman didn't recite any substance. There was also no evidence on the scene. Steve Horning also had a record in the year 1970.

He was detained in connection with assaulting female investigator. We weren't certain whether Patsy was aware of this, however, she already had a relative run an identity check on Steve at the time that their financial troubles began. She probably knew. However, Steve as well as Sally Horning fully cooperated with the police investigation as well as a private investigator.

Steve actually had two polygraphs, while the first failed to conclude. He was successful on the second. Evidently, these tests are not admissible before a judge however it's an intriguing footnote. In the case, Detective Gustafson also received a threatening phone call a few months during the course of the probe. The man who claimed did anyone know Leo fixe had a relationship with Linda Donahue?

Linda Donahue is a 41 year old woman that was murdered at her apartment in Arlington in the month of June 1987, which was just five months after Patsy's death. She was stabbed and strangled. What is the significance of this? Leo fixe as well as Patsy had a brief relationship for a time before she left her after seven or eight months. prior to her death. fixe was an undergraduate student of Southern Methodist university where he was a chemistry student. Gustafson discovered that he purchased a product in 1987's summer from the sole store that sold strychnine. Dallas flex had met Patsy prior to her wedding with Bob Cox.

After their divorce the couple separated, he began to seek for her again in 1984. The couple had split up him in the past because he was dating other people, however, they returned to their relationship at the beginning of the year 1987. The second time Patsy was able to end the relationship. He pushed her to marry she had gone through two divorces, and was no desire to marry again.

He told Gustafson that he was shocked and said I wondered when you going to come to me. When the detective called him as the others before him. Leo fixe was able to pass a polygraph. It was discovered that the company from which he purchased chemicals from Solar Products to clean up services, not strychnine, and it wasn't on the invoice.

Additionally, flex was not looked into in connection with the Linda Donna Hughes murder. Because they only had been for a couple of days after the murder the man identified as Roger Eugene Frane jr. Was identified via DNA. He was already in jail for a murder that was similar to his. Investigators were at a dead-end. However, Gustafson was able to identify a suspect that who he liked because Patsy more intelligent. Her ex spouse, Bob Cox, several of her relatives and friends have made statements about Cox.

Then of course then there's the restraining orders that Patsy was able to obtain. The woman told her friends, she was followed by him, he watched her and was threatening to end her life. It was actually the reason she put in security measures on her rental property. It is not expensive and usually not a concern when it comes to a short-term rental.

It was even more fascinating is the divorce they had. Bob did not have a lot of assets, and he had five pending lawsuits against his former business partners. He wasn't likely to get any money from the estate of Patsy however, revenge was not going to be handed out. The predatory behaviour and his nefarious behavior was an issue, but the evidence was only circumstantial.

Remember that fire that destroyed Galveston at the museum of wax, he had been awarded an Patsy to purchase. He then sued Hartford Lloyd's insurance company for refusing to acknowledge his claim. He claimed that hobos were responsible for the fire, however the insurance company claimed that Cox himself was the one who set the fire in order in order to collect insurance proceeds. Cox had not been able convince his wife to buying the museum in disrepair.

In reality, she offered him $14,000, but he was insulted that he had declined. The insurance was $300,000. Strangely, this didn't alter their relationship and Patsy was actually able to give an interview to Hartford during the civil case he was pursuing. She spoke with Hartford at least 10 times between 1986 and 1987, focusing on the value of the house in the manner she had it appraised.

Her position was of harm her husband's lawsuit. Evidently, Patsy was aware about the fact that one of her most precious items at the museum was transferred to Bob's office in Garland, Texas before the fire. Patsy was to appear in the lawsuit in November 1987 just 10 days after her loss of life. In the end, Bob Cox won his lawsuit however.

Hartford could demonstrate that not all the valuable objects were destroyed. It was impossible to prove that he started the fire. The jury awarded him $1.3 million. Perhaps Bob Cox, wasn't willing to take on his ex-wife who was a respected and reputable citizen, to stand against him. Patsy Wright wasn't only an ordinary socialite.

She was a well-known businesswoman and was in was in the same industry of museums as her husband and testimony from her could be a reason for him to lose the trial. There's more Bob Cox all, but refused to testify regarding the death of his ex-wife He was reported to have said that he had have met her, I got married to her and divorced her. He also refused an examination by polygraph.

The sole additional suspect for the killing of Patsy Bolton Wright. Was that a student Stanley Lester pointer. The man who was detained for stealing souvenirs from wreckage of the Southwest wax museum. It is interesting to note that the object that he was found in was a financial ledger for the business. Private investigator, Bill Deere was able to identify this as alarming as he may have given away several thousand dollars' worth of artifacts in order to take that ledger off the shelf.

Deere claimed that the suspect was in search of materials to blackmail. However, Stanley pointer was killed in the head by a cop on April 13 the 13th of April, 1991. He struck the policeman who was sitting on by the highway making an arrest warrant. The officer slid off the car's front and hit the hood. Pointer began to steer the carin an attempt to knock the officer off but the policemen held on to the car and shot him several times in the windscreen. Stanley pointer did not run because he was clipping the officer.

Two warrants for felony arrest were issued that were issued in connection to another arson incident at our girls young center back in the month of December 1990. That's very likely to be a coincidence. Could there be an association to Cox as well as pointer? Someone claimed that Galveston fire could have been a factor, even if it was not proven, and someone certainly lit a fire in the Southwest wax museum. No one has ever been charged for the murder of Patsy Wright.

It doesn't appear that anyone else will ever get to be the victim of this case. includes suspicious family members, the trainers of horses in their forest inspection along with a mysterious fire the vengeful ex-husband of Sally Horning collection of her sister's quote. She was a gorgeous sophisticated, intelligent and elegant woman who was willing to go the extra mile to make people feel at ease.

People loved her and thought about her. She had no enemies. Sally Horning was right about her sister in the beginning part, and by all accounts, Patsy Bolton Wright. Was an extraordinary woman however she was wrong regarding her adversaries. The list of those who can benefit either directly or in indirect ways from the death of Patsy Cline is staggering.

Sometimes. The most straightforward answer is always the best. I would say Bob Cox, her ex husband, is one of the suspects, and He had the trifecta motives, love of and money as well as revenge.

Chapter 2: Upstairs Lounge Fire

On the day of pride on June 24 1973, a brand new Orleans gay bar known as the upstairs lounge was engulfed in flames within a short period between two and three minutes. The cause was arsonist 29. The fire claimed the lives of a number of people and three letters were afflicted with their injuries at the hospital. It was the deadliest fire ever recorded in New Orleans however, it was not the only one to die within the first few days.

There was no help from the city's officials or the Louisiana governor or even from churches. There was no sympathy offered. Many churches do not want to bury the deceased, however homosexuals gathered to the survivors. The event is usually regarded as to be the beginning of the movement for game rights in the city of New Orleans but, there was an official investigation conducted by police and the Fire Marshall however, nobody was ever taken into custody and the investigation was finally closed in 1980.

In spite of the terrible tragedy the fire was just buried in history for a long time. However, in recent times historians have been thinking about how to provide light and understanding to this tragedy which has caused such pain to the LGBTQ community of New Orleans.

It is located at the bend of the Mississippi river. New Orleans. Louisiana is an Gulf of Mexico busiest port since the 17th century. It was named the Crescent city due to the fact that the first town was constructed on the crest of a sharp bend into the river. It was designed to resemble the Crescent moon. New Orleans is world famous for its Creole food and its distinctive dialect.

In addition, as the home of jazz music when America warring, New Orleans of the civil war Orleans is the sole location in America that slaves were permitted to have their own drums. When European drums were first introduced at the end of the 19th century, Voodoo-inspired rhythms mingled with horns became the norm in new Orleans bar spaces.

The vibrant style of jazz brought people joy and at ease. New Orleans is forever influenced by its European history. Louisiana was repeatedly fought between French and Spanish in the 17th century until United States bought it in 1803. The word Creole was first utilized by French colonists to English.

The people were born in Louisiana or from people who have migrated to. It is believed that the Creole language is regarded as a mixture from English, French, and Spanish. There are believed to be over a hundred distinct Creole dialects beginning from the 15th century, although most people consider the primary creole dialect to be French. Creole as being French. Since France established Louisiana in the early 1800s, modern Orleans has taken on the lively culture that is Creole culture.

In all aspects there is nothing quite like an entirely modern Orleans accent however. People are trying to make comparisons to other dialects of the region. There is nothing quite like Creole food that is influenced by European colonists, yet built on the distinctive seafood available to the region. New Orleans Creole cuisine draws people who love food from across the globe.

I'm almost salivating over the crawfish and jumbalaya at TFA. The way I describe this is a new Orleans has another name, which is big, easy , for its 24/7 nightlife that is accompanied by the music of jazz flowing out into areas from the bars and revelers are free to wander in the French quarter. Bourbon Street is today the top tourist attraction within new Orleans in which beads drop from balconies to crowds of people reveling beneath locals and tourists alike.

Get ready for celebrations and festivals, the most particularly Mardi Gras, but also Southern decadence, which is a gay pride celebration. The past 100 years of New Orleans history have been shattered by tensions between people of different races, the racial divide, poverty, and natural catastrophes. Katrina, a Category Five hurricane that struck the Gulf coast in 2005. Katrina is a deadly category five hurricane, that hit the city between June in August 2005, caused massive destruction, killing more than 2000 people, and displaces over a million within that Gulf coastal region.

New Orleans in the early 1970s was the result of the other events happening in the United States. It was also the time of the Watergate scandal and the ending of the Vietnam war. Numerous social changes were achieved through black power and women's liberation movements. The important ruling that was made by Roe V. Wade gave women federally protected rights in their body for the very first time.

The beginning of the seventies was strongly influenced by the popular culture of the latter sixties. Hippies were enthralled by Timothy Leary's motto of tune to the tune and then dropping out. They did it in waves. The drug culture became more sombre and more widespread during the 1970s. In June 1969 the Stonewall protests at New York kicked off the gay rights movement.

The riots consisted of violent and spontaneous demonstrations of gay, lesbian, and transgender communities as a result of an arrest by police in the Stonewall Inn and Greenwich village. The LGBTQ community had endured for years of harassment, discrimination of police brutality, discrimination, and discrimination, and had finally fought to defend themselves.

Today, the gay pride month June Pride Day, which falls on June 24, but parades and celebrations continue for weeks across the country, beginning in the year 1970 and continuing until today. What started as a vital campaign for gay people to be restored to their dignity equality and to be acknowledged as a part of America is now an opportunity to celebrate diversity and love.

New Orleans also had a reputation of tolerance but it wasn't always well-deserved. There over 20 bars that were gay within the French quarter in the era, however lawful sodomy was still in place and the gay community was under the threat of police raids however, it was in the French quarter and not every of the new Orleans that was more welcoming towards the gay community.

Also called The VU Caray, meaning the old square. The area was established in the 18th century by French or Spanish colonists, with an extraordinary number of people who were free of color. Maybe this is the reason why the culture of tolerance was established. There were people of every race lived and worked in the same place. It was just a matter time before gay people began to flock to a secure location such as this.

However, despite being accepting, there were severe laws in place to discriminate against homosexuals. Johnny Townsend pointed out that there were thirteen arrests and four beatings in January alone in 1971. like every other year, gender-neutral and feminine males were often the target. Gay men flocked to each other and in private spaces, often referred to as"tea rooms," which actually bathrooms.

The most popular cruising area in people in French area was Cabrini park, and male hustlers worked in numerous gay bars throughout the quarter. While many of these bars were geared towards people who hustled and Johns When 39-year-old Phil was able to decide to create an establishment for gays in the year the year 1970. He was sure to create an acceptable establishment.

Phil was introduced to his bartender and manager his buddy. Rasmusson in a gay-friendly bar in Iberville known as the Tavern. Phil hired him right away and he was open and gay man. He was during his time in the military and after he was caught by another person and confessed to his commander and was dismissed. When he returned to home in Texas He decided that to never conceal his sexuality for a second time.

He was fired from several jobs as he was always honest with prospective employers upfront. He wasn't employed for six months after moving to New Orleans however, quickly he found success in a bar that served drinks to gay men. Phil and his buddy began to work on rehabilitating the space. Phil was the one who chose it to build it on the 2nd floor in an older three-story building that was located at the intersection between charters as well as Iberville within the Quarter.

It wasn't a particularly popular spot to have a bar with walk-in customers, as it was difficult to draw customers on the second floor. Phil and his partner set up a canopy near the entry point and stairwell. The stairwell was able to read upstairs on two sides inviting patrons to climb the stairs straight away. The guys found the entryway into the stairwell inconvenient.

It was carpeted, and 13 steps that were twisted through ugly pipe. They carpeted the stairs and then hung the fabric. Covering the walls with wallpaper to hide the pipes, creating an even more welcoming space to be in. Inside there were three rooms. The first, which is 40 feet across and 20 feet high, has four windows that overlook Iberville street, and three windows overlooking charters.

The massive Archway was a doorway to another room which was 16 feet long and featured three windows that overlooked the charter street. It was also dark due to the fact that the three windows were darkly painted. It also had a fire protected door that led onto the roof of the next building. All the windows were nine feet high with sashes which were raisedto let in breezes during the summer heat.

However, by the year 1970 the building was controlled as the tenant before had placed bars on the windows to protect them from falling. to ensure that if the windows were opened, one could leap into the air and tumble. Therefore, it's quite understandable. Another issue is that the lack of a balcony. Balconies are everywhere within the Quarter. Nearly every bar, lounge or hotel has one on the upper floors, designed as places to hang out and take in the air.

Balconies also played a role in security in case of fire. If an upstairs room was fitted with balconies, experts consider that the death of a person would have been much lower than it was. Also, Phil thought that windows ruined the intimate atmosphere they were trying to create. They wanted a quiet space. Therefore, they screened off the windows in the bar area in the first space and all the windows in the second The design for the bar sort of decided already with the orange and pink laminate that was used to cover the bar.

There was red flocked wallpaper and outdoor red indoor carpeting all over. There was no way to avoid the vibrant colors. They sat on them , draped fabric over flaws. Beefcake prints of the day graced the walls such as the famous, one featuring naked Burt Reynolds on a bear skin rug. One of his friends even purchased white clothing, which was popular in the era, and tie dyed it both orange and pink.

They constructed a platform in the corner of their room, and placed an old piano that was white on top of it in the middle room. They raised a platform to serve as dance floors. The upstairs bar became the only gay-friendly bar in New Orleans to obtain the license to dance. The public touching of the same sexe was not permitted.

Naturally, dancing. Most likely, it wasn't. It's important to remember that even though Phil and his pals did everything they could to make the area beautiful, they made sure to adhere to all fire codes. The store's entrance was replaced by a fire-rated doors, while two more fire exits were built.

A similar one was mentioned inside the 3rd room however another was built into an opening close to the main entryway. The window was not barred, and opened to the fire escape, but the fire escape did not have the ladder needed to reach the floor. In its place, were steps that led into the 3rd floor. Just fill it up and adhere to fire code.

He made open invitations to the vice-team. He had to tell Terman to ensure that the bar wouldn't be a place only for hustlers but also discouraged drag queens. At first, a narcotics police officer was looking around the bar. I was so impressed that I was a regular, and even brought the wife of his, Betty. Also, anyone who had sex in the bathroom was thrown out.

Phil was aware that he could not fully control that however, he did his best. He did his best. The upstairs lounge opened to the public on Halloween 1970. It was also the year that the first costume party took place. however, bar owners had several loyal patrons, the business was slow because of the place.

Buddy was the one who came up with the idea of host an annual beer bust.

They would charge fifty cents and they were aware that it was the only drink you could consume between five and 7:00 pm on Sundays. When you got to the end of the day, you returned your mug home and exchanged at 50 cents. You could basically consume all the drinks you want at a cost of just a dollar. They were hoping that people would remain after the party and pay the regular price.

It did the trick. The bear bus actually went off and attracted hundreds of more people every Sunday. Phil hired a man whose name was David, Gary affectionately, called piano, Dave to entertain the crowd on beer buses. The music would always turn into singalongs and Dave finished the weekly beer bust with a rousing rendition of United.

Standing patrons gathered in a circle with pride, watching the first song to be famous by the manhood and later Sonny as well as Cher. It was a daily ritual that was adored by the frequent visitors. The upstairs was also the venue for Mardi Gras parties, Easter Bonnet Contests, and hilariously funny try sickle races with a buddy. was not just a top professional, but also a charming and cheerful bartender.

He used to call everyone sweetheart or honey, and tried his best to make people feel at in the same space following having enjoyed the popularity of the bus as well as other events, buddy, and Phil bell , who staged in the rear of the third space, Betty the wife of the cop. Along with other regulars, they helped get an intimate theater group up and running and putting on shows dubbed Nellie dramas. The the cross-dressing and cleverly disguised laughter really made the audience laugh.

Soon. They were placing popcorn on the tables in the room, and people could throw the popcorn at him every time the stage was set. Although Phil initially had averted drag shows, their popularity was increasing and he could not ignore the benefits of hosting. The shows. The first drag performer upstairs was Marcy Marcel , born in the year of his birth. Marcos Grandio.

She would perform to the stage around 8:00 PM an hour following the bar's beer bust or theatre shows. One of the regulars at the bar was the Reverend bill Larson who was a member of the Metropolitan Community Church. The MCC was established in 1968 in LA by Reverend Troy Perry to minister to the gay community. It was a branch with branch offices located with branches in Atlanta, New York and Nashville.

The new Orleans branch was established in 1970 which coincided with the opening of an upstairs lounge. The church was first situated in a small house situated on Elysian fields Avenue, but when Reverend Larson was appointed to replace the previous pastor, he realized the church needed the best location. He visited Philistine and asked if he could have Sunday services at the beginning of the week prior to the beer bus's arrival.

Phil acknowledged the idea. The initial MCC Sunday worship service took place on the 19th of Monday 1971. The congregation grew accustomed to staying late after services to take advantage of the beer bus. They eventually did raise the funds to purchase the property they owned. In the following months the tradition of having afternoon drinks in the upstairs bar was carried on maybe because of the MCCs influence in the bar The production of the theater began to reap the benefits of donations being made to children with disabilities and the poor.

The upstairs lounge was the place Phil had envisioned as to be a Haven for gay people that was a place where gay people from both races could gather. Gay guys could have dates, and straight people were at ease. The warmth of the regulars as well as the everyone else who gathered in the bar was amazing. The welcoming atmosphere upstairs made the tragic event even more painful.

In the morning of the 24th of June, the day of pride in 1973, Marcy Marcel woke with the feeling of fear. It wasn't just her who felt this way. be the first to share a premonition. Townson documents, numerous accounts of people who had an unpleasant feeling in the days before and following day after the fire an underlying fear that danger was approaching or they were about to say goodbye to someone whom they'd never meet again. It was a scorching morning in the third quarter and there were no storms in that afternoon to chill things down.

It is common to have an afternoon storm. You could set your alarm clock on the storms. But that day, Marci chose to stay in the air conditioner and never ventured out of her house the next day. Normally, she would get dressed and head out early to catch the conclusion of the bust in beer, but because of something that caused her to stay in the house, even when it was at the very last minute, she chose to sit and sit through the first minutes of an Betty Davis movie that was showing at 8:00 pm.

She was scheduled to perform at the time, however, she I thought it was okay to be in the back. It was just one time. Buddy. His lover, Adam got to the bar around noon however, he needed to settle the till from the previous night making it a deposit and then let the bar open for the bust of a beer. Adam was able to create the appearance of a British accent to conceal his Creole accent.

He was ashamed to admit that he his addiction to alcohol that he was ashamed of it. It was a serious issue however, his friend loved him and cared for his needs. He gave Adam his first drink around 22:00 pm. Adam always was at the back of the bar, looking over his the bar with his friend, and was loved by the others who frequented the bar, Phil. It seems that Steve wasn't in the bar on that day. He left to make sure the couple could see the damn Yankees in The Beverly dinner Playhouse though.

It was Pride Day. It was not celebrated in New Orleans or at the upper levels however it was the typical Sunday afternoon crowd made up of MCC members as well as other regulars who attended the bust of beer. The bus departed promptly at 5:45 PM, and a friend later reported that 90 people attended on the day.

The bust was over the crowd began to thin out to around 60 core regulars at 7:15 PM.

After the bust was over, piano, Dave stepped down and the next player took over Matt. He awoke to end the evening, but. Dave was hanging out and chatting with his friends but the bus was not running smoothly the previous day. There was an unidentified, young, dark-haired man who was positioned in the bathroom, without Phil's knowledge.

A hole was drilled between the bathroom toilets. The man was causing trouble for patrons by making sexually explicit remarks throughout the entire incident. The rogue named Michael Scarborough, reported him to his buddy and another bartender Hugh Cooley, sometime between 630 and 7:15 at night. They forced him off the toilet, and asked that he should leave the bar.

The man was furious at angry at this. Michael walked over to his table to confront Michael was finally up and struck his jaw in anger, sending him down, and then spotting the fighting buddy along with Hugh through the dark-haired man's door and another disturbance was created by a man of long, dark blonde hair. He would take empty mugs, and then nag patrons who had pitchers to get refills.

He was repeatedly warned about this, and after the beer bust was over He swarmed around the area, looking for cash, hoping to claim the 50 cents deposits. But the police caught him and ordered the man to leave. When he left, he was a mess. He grabbed two mugs, smashing them on the floor on the stool. Then, you went downstairs to clean up, you found the broken glass was there, and your buddy was cleaning up his workspace just about to leave, and you took over for the evening.

He was at work from noon until his shift came to an end at 8:15 pm. Adam and Adam had plans for dinner with a different car. Reggie as well as Regina, Reggie Regina have one of the most heart-warming love stories I have read in both books. Both were from religious backgrounds. When they met one another it was definitely a romance match.

Regina The real name of his was Ricky Salito, but she was a woman. She was a woman and

Reggie which name she should pick for herself. He explained to her that his name was, Reginald Matt King, and advised her to be Regina since they were his queen. Regina was white while Reggie was black, and she would later claim that there were not many safe inter-racial areas.

The couple had the option of leaving. She stated, quote, we felt like we were at home upstairs. The couple was seated next to the piano, along with their companion who was a straight white woman called Jean Gosnell the piano Dave another straight woman called Arnaz Brown who was with her two sons who were gay and some others who were regulars. As Reggie was aware of the situation, the conversation was over, he said he didn't have enough money to eat dinner and had to go back to his apartment to pick up the checkbook.

However, Regina said, not really, you requested drinks. The house was 5 minutes walk away. The girl kissed Reggie and then said, I'll return in ten minutes. She never saw Reggie again. In the evening, at 7:53 an elderly woman was living just across the street from the bar was walking towards the corner of Walgreens located on Iberville along with Royal.

Then she was listening to a woman yell fire. She turned her back and saw flames in the stairwell to the upper level. She ran to the bar in the midship next door. She told the bartender that she needed assistance. The fire department recorded the phone call and dispatched the call at 7:56 PM. The lounge at the time had buzzers for deliveries during the day and taxi drivers to check it as they picked up customers right at seven fifty, and then, around two or threetimes, it began buzzing non-stop.

Nobody knows, until today, what caused it, or who may have been responsible. However, the irritated buddy and asked a patron nearby. He was asked if he could investigate the door, he could force the person to stop. Luther Boggs was a favorite frequent visitor, who was always ready to lend a hand. He went to the door and then opened it. The flames immediately forced him to go forward.

The fire was ablaze. Even though the door was equipped with fire protection, specifically to be in compliance with the fire codes. The spring mechanism broke and the door broke open the stairwell and drew oxygen from the upstairs area which created the effect of a chimney that pushed the flames towards the bar in a matter of seconds. The carpeting and drapes, the wallpaper Everything was smoldering.

It happened so fast. A lot of people were sat in stunned silence. A customer, who was near the entrancewas struck by the floor. The moment the fire erupted and he was able to get to the side window , which had no bars. He sat on a chair , and broken the glass. He ran down the fire escape and was terrified. After he realized there was no ladder there was already a large crowd of people watching and screaming for him to jump.

He was also on the fire. The bar patron from the midship served an ice-cold pitcher onto him in order to put out the fire. Luther Bogs along with Jean Gosnell were right on his heels. The gene was nervous and was moving slowly. Therefore, Luther was pushed by her, breaking one of her teeth. When they reached the escape route, they both were in flames and attempted to put the flames onto one another.

He snuffed the fire in the gene, but was still burning. He jumped to the ground , the man put water over the top of his head. There are horrifying images of Luther lying on the stretcher. The skin is dripping off his body. He clearly screams and is screaming in pain. Gene was afraid to leap. So she climbed the stairs to the 3rd floor, waiting for rescue She would be able to survive and be admitted to the hospital for a series of operations, amputations, and skin transplants Luther.

Her friend who was her best friend died at the hospital. The bar was full of chaos. One couple who was watching the fight in the exits made the decision to jump straight into the blazed staircase together. Amazingly, both survived, albeit with serious burns. Until then, the majority of patrons could not get to the exit for fire escape which Luther and his companions had traversed because it was far enough from the stairs.

Buddy was aware of the third insurance company and quickly acted. He began to call people on his shoulder screaming, Come with Me, come along with me. However, many were to be scared and confused, which included Adam, his love. Adam. The couple remained afloat on the Barstool however, he ended eventually leading a group around 20 people away from danger the next night.

A man called Duane Mitchell, aka Mitch was part of the group. When he stepped out and took a look around, he discovered his beloved Horace was still in the Inferno. He ran back to the Inferno to save Horace. The bodies of the victims were later discovered burned together. After the buddy had got the bodies out of the way and on the roof next to them and they started climbing through one of the windows of the apartment and then walked back onto the road.

They looked at the flame and were shocked to take their loved ones to the water, and then suffer with the flames. Four people managed to get down the fire escape around 20 in the morning, and then escaped with their friends which left about 35-40 people trying to get out. They were pulling drapes down, and pulling shutters from windows however security bars were getting in the way.

There are people who manage to slip through bars. One of them was old Quintin who was employed as bar back. The iconic photo of him lying on the floor, crying and gazing towards the fire. The caption of the photograph states what the man was crying over. My friends are there. He was in the crowd caring for the injured and urging people to jump. A young man by the name of Francis de Frain, made it through the bars, and afterwards, he recited the story of Clayton Delery Edward's quote.

If you were overweight it was considered a problem. I wasn't, thanks to you God. He was admitted to an emergency room two weeks later, suffering from third degree burns covering a lot of his body even his facial. Michael Scarborough, the guy who hit the man who was in the street, was able to get through the bars. His arms, face and hands were badly burned.

The Reverend bill Larson of the MCC was also at the bar that night. He was pushing the air conditioner out trying to escape through the window. But he got caught in bars. He was heard shouting Oh God, no. As his family and friends below watched him die to death in pain You can view the body of his victim in photos hanging half-way out of the window.

It's a horrifying and horrifying image. Three others were burned alive in the same window as the man, however. One man's shoe was visible. Photos of people who were on the ground watched the people trapped pushed their bodies on the glass. However, he could see Adam clearly sitting on his Barstool with his arms raised and screaming. his arms.

He was eventually tossed down by the stream of an hose of fire. Virgina took only 10 minutes. She told herself she'd be there, at the time she was walking back, the downstairs was completely flooded. She was crying and tried to get up to the firefighter, but he stood in her way and her lover was eagerly waiting to meet me. She exclaimed. She was finally told by someone that no one who had been near the piano been able to get out.

Regina claims she doesn't remember anything else after the incident. Even the following two months were terrifying blank in her mind. The fire was put out at 8:12 pm. It took only 16 minutes since the call for assistance was recorded. And 29 people were dead. Police arrived to manage the crowds and start their investigation.

However, he continued to provide assistance wherever he could, and also comfort his fellow acquaintances. He noticed the dark-haired young man. He had thrown his hands out and grabbed his arm leading the man to a policeman but the officer would not take him seriously and demanded that he let go. Journalists from TV and print were at the scene, and it was the Times Picayune photographer Ronnie LeBoeuf who took the most shocking photos from the evening.

His journalist colleagues, Clancy, Dubose. He was sent to the Picayune to a hospital for charity or for the injured to be transferred. He recalled the horrific screaming of pain as well as the smell of burnt flesh. The next day, he wrote in his front-page article, the infant unit was to be opened in two weeks. When the director of the charity was alerted of the flames, he requested that it be opened immediately.

15 people were transported to the hospital, some with minor injuries however, many had to stay for weeks or months recovering from more serious injuries.

The firefighters on the at the scene became sick by sight and smells, and were forced to stop frequently. They were later criticised for leaving bodies, such as Bill Larson's, in plain view which they had to. Moving the bodies was a gruelling task , and many were blamed with a slap and towards one another. It was also extremely difficult to get around.

Investigators also had to capture everything prior to when any person could be relocated.

Three bodies were discovered near the restroom or within the area. A few were discovered around the piano, as well as scattered throughout the bar. 17 people were found piled in a clump against the windows. They were the ones who had been suffering in pain through the windows, and by the people below.

When removing the bodies, investigators discovered seven-ounce cans of lighter fluid near the lower part of the staircase. The survivor contacted the Reverend Troy Perry in Los Angeles to let him know the details of what happened. Arson was suspected immediately because the churches of LA and Nashville were burned until the floor.

Flowers were left by the location but they would later be taken. An older black man named smokey was appointed as the guardian. He was a former convict and straight. However, the folks upstairs always shown him respect. He also told journalists that he was unable to pay for his own flowers, but could help the ones that others had left.

Troy Perry and his team scheduled a press conference the next day, June 25th. They criticised the police and city officials over their actions or inactions and set up the creation of a Memorial for the evening of 8:15 pm. Perry as well as his crew tried to find a church to host the Memorial. I was repeatedly denied.

I watched him on the film upstairs at Ferno Street. Charges were stowed at him. They hanged up on himand laughing at his jokes and hung up on him. Finally, Father Bill Richardson from St. George's Episcopal church offered his church to host the June 25th Memorial. The church was under intense scrutiny, not just by his bishop, but also from the congregation as well, one woman said.

She refused to return to St. George's until the priests performed an exorcism. A. The Episcopal archbishop from Louisiana phoned Richardson in protest of his anger and to discuss Richardson who reportedly said do you believe Jesus might have had the courage to keep them out of the church? Richardson was furious in writing an open note to his church about the criticism.

If a large portion of St. George members believe that the church's mission is a place to serve only the few who are in it and not the whole population I'll think about resigning as your pastor in the near time. The Bishop and vestry may search for a new rector. The Bishop did not have to step down. The letter was highly powerful.

Catholic archbishop Phillip Hannon, cowered away from making a statement. He told his secretary to constantly say there was no the office. However, he continued to release statements on other issues. He didn't go to the hospital for charity. He didn't attend memorials, or any of the funerals. Unfortunately, Catholic victims weren't given the full Catholic funerals.

A priest who was not named performed several ceremonies, but he refused to claim the entire Catholic rights. Johnny Townson named his book. Let the faggots go to roost following what was reportedly heard on the scene. One firefighter said that we couldn't climb up to the top. The fire was burning to save people one fireman reportedly said"Oh fuck it!.

It's just flaggots. Let them go to waste. There's no way to verify that the incident took place. Townson does not identify the survivor who heard the incident However, considering the attitudes that were prevalent at the day, it shouldn't be a surprise. VU, Caray commissioner Wayne take a stand against criticism and blame the Fire Marshall's office. In reality the fire marshals had been conducting the most thorough investigation.

They arrived on the scene within 5 minutes. Two other major fires that had occurred in recent times that received an outpouring of support from the public, even official mornings, in which people declared, specifically, for a fire which had claimed the lives of police officers at Howard Johnson's resort. It was true that the new Orleans officials, churches as well as the governor spoke out about these previous tragedies.

Bishop Hannon performed funerals and was present of the deceased, notably policemen who were involved. The funerals would not be like the funerals for the governor's office. Governor. Edwin Edwards, only public statements stated that he would advocate for changes to the code of fire. Edwards never expressed condolences nor expressed any sympathy to the survivors and victims of the fire that erupted upstairs.

The mayor moon Landro was more adamant. The mayor made a statement that said that the victims were difficult to recognize because, quote, some of the thieves were in the bar and, you know, it was a gay bar, and it was common for homosexuals to have fake IDs. This was untrue. the majority of bartenders and police officers agreed that the only ones who had fake IDs were minor age and AMA the outright defiance of those in the government who obliterated the horrors that the humors of.

What is the biggest tragedy that took place in the city of New Orleans on the 24th of June, that was the day that 30 faggots were killed, and not many more. Did you catch the story of the burning Queens? One of the worst for what some people had to say about the church that was refusing to offer Christian burials. What they did was to quote their fruit that were placed in jars of fruit, however there were many new Orleaneans that were willing to take the initiative.

Townsend spoke of Jim Roberts, the mortician who prepared and embalmed Jayne Mansfield's funeral during June 1967. Jim Roberts worked at Boltman funeral homes, where he provided time and services to many unclaimed bodies , and also donated grave plots, coffins, and coffins. The initial Memorial was very modest with just 35 people present. and the reverend Troy Perry declared a day of mourning for July 1st. He then began making plans for a larger Memorial.

They were unable to find a church that would organize a ceremony. Then they NCC discovered an Methodist church that was willing to host the Memorial. The church was headed by a black pastor , and an area of the town that was black. It was the pastor Edward

Kennedy had reached out to the MCC and invited his church to participate. The MCC was printing 3000 flyers to distribute to Memorial people who were walking along the streets.

Sometimes, they wouldn't even accept the flyer, fearing not even showing an interest would be enough without them. However, the NCC and the gay community was impressed when small-sized businesses within this quarter that are not only gay-owned, placed the flyers on their doors The Methodist bishop of Louisiana Venice Crutchfield attended the Memorial in order to show her support for the ministers of color, Edward Kennedy who allowed the Memorial however, he also took care of himself in later years that he wanted to be gay and come out.

It's not difficult to discern the motivation of his today however he took an huge risk when he didn't have the item of the state. The Times Picayune put the number at between two to 300 people were at the Memorial. There was no way to know for certain. The Reverend Troy Perry led the service. Other pastors also spoke. were led by Knowles toward the conclusion.

Perry declared, quote, We are thankful to people such as Reverend Kennedy as well as Bishop Crutchfield who are able to stand up for us in this moment. He then passed around the lyrics printed on paper of United. We are as the unofficial Anthem in the lounge upstairs and led the crowd to sing towards the close. Someone handed Perry an email notifying him that, contrary to his earlier promises, that the media wouldn't be present.

The camera crews were stationed at the entrance of the insurance. He stood and warned mourners. A lot of gay people aren't gay and have plenty to lose were noticed suddenly. According to the legend, a mysterious woman was seen standing on the balcony and wept. Yes, I'm proud of my identity and who my friends are. I entered the front door, and I'm going to leave in this way.

Perry was directing the mourners to a discreet side door which let them out into the alleyway. In addition, according to legend, everyone in the church walked straight out through the doorway in front. The testimony of Johnny Townsend's book say they did see some people sneak through the side doors. I'm sure this is true. as there were a lot of witnesses that could have contradicted Perry However, I believe there were people who were legitimately scared were pushed out by the side entrance and blamed them.

They were traumatized, so beaten, and now they were terrified from being added their families and employers on TV. Following the memorials, the investigation began in earnest by the NOPD as well as the Fire Marshall and coroner were assigned distinct duties. The NOPD is allegedly investigating the commission of a crime.

However, their investigation was not as thorough and they ultimately resigned from the fire. Marshall was more concerned with identifying the crime, along with Loring who was interested in the cause and the ways it could have been prevented. The coroner was simply trying to find the bodies. The Fire Marshall found there was no evidence that any of the exits to the fire were insufficient.

In actual fact, they discovered that the door to the fire, but the way he guided over 20 people through, had saved lives and fulfilled its goal. The fire chief was quoted as saying it was not his belief that victims had died from burning, but that they died of carbon monoxide resulting from the smoke, but that witnesses were able to watch the scene as bill Larson and his fellow victims burn to death in pain.

His words were an insult for the people who witnessed the horror unfold. The victims were loved ones and friends burning to death in front of their own eyes. The majority of victims were so badly burned by the fire that their identification was delayed for weeks and three weeks before they were to be identified. The MCC attempted to bring these bodies Barre city ordinances that stated they were only released to relatives and refused to release the bodies for burial in the Church.

The unidentified men were laid to rest in pauper's plots and graves that were not marked. The majority of victims needed to be identified using jewelry. In one instance, the tattoo was remarkably buried beneath the skin's outer layer. Regina her lover was recognized through jewelry because they couldn't marry. Regina had given Reggie the ring she received from her High School, and the ring remained in his possession until he died.

She also said that the victim was buried. The victim had been dentist. Perry waters was not an outcast in his field, however, he was a member of the community and was frequently treated gays with no insurance or funds. His secretary provided us with dental records when he did not arrive at work the following day.

She also released many documents to help identify the deceased. Although many funerals were held in the MCC. There were many more who were in despair as families of the victims did not allow them to be released. They would also not take the victims.

Reverend bill Larson's mother was embarrassed. She was unable to take the body of her son, even though.

Then she released her body into her MCC and they arranged for his remains to be burned. He was buried in an urn, and they used it as their church until a congregation offered a funeral tomb, however his name doesn't appear on the exterior witness description from his buddy. Other witnesses in the bar pointed out the dark-haired man in the bathroom, or the blonde male trying to steal mugs both were removed prior to the fire started.

The crowd was trying to figure out an explanation, but the majority of people believed it was the dark-haired man. He did however give a lengthy description the events of the day. He also gave an account of both men, even though the policeman forced him to allow the dark haired man to go. He was found and taken to the police station for questioning around 4:00 am that day.

The clerk in the corner of Walgreens was quizzed and she was able to recall selling a bottle that contained lighter fluid for a person with black hair whom she regarded as homosexual due to his manner of speaking. She stated that he appeared unhappy, evidently drinking, and his hands were shaking. He asked for the tiniest four-ounce can however they were not available.

She had to offer them the seven-ounce can the fire and police investigators had spoken to the young man Alan Godrey, who had been present at the scene of the fire . He told them he knew the dark haired guy who was kicked off the premises on that night. The name of the man was Roger Nunez. When the police were able to investigate him, he appeared like he was drunk.

Then he said he'd recently experienced seizures of epileptic origin. The police took him to the hospital for charity for a check-up. Doctors discovered that there was a fractured jaw and the police realized they needed to find someone who had suffered the same injury. Because Michael Scarborough had said that he punched him on the jaw. Doctors carried out surgery to fix the jaw, and then wired his teeth to keep it in the correct position.

The police had to leave Nunez in the hospital without guards, and requested that they contact the detectives, before releasing the patient seven days later on the seventh of July. Investigators went to talk with Nunez at the hospital and discovered that he was released. In spite of the note in his file that he was discharged, they spent the following two days looking for the gene Davis who was the owner of the bar that was a hideaway Nunez.

His boss claimed that he was sitting on the fender of his vehicle in the evening, just looking out onto the streets. But he didn't spot anyone. If he were the location he claimed to be then he would have witnessed the perpetrator , and he would see people fleeing from the flames. Davis added that when the fire was started that he witnessed Nunez appear out of the corner Royal the canal street.

And when he arrived at the bar that was hidden away and sat down, he said, Thank God I was able to get out of the fire , as like he was trying to claim that there was a fire in the upstairs area when the fire first started. No one else had seen him return. Then, after being thrown out on July 15 when the new Orleans fire department finally made a public statement, saying that it was arson.

In the course of his interview, Michael Scarborough was interviewed at the hospital on the 17th of July and he gave another information about Nunez . He claimed that after he hit him. Nunez reportedly declared, I'm going take you all out of the detectives. Scarborough to review the photo line-up. Then he chose Nunez from eight mugshots that Scarborough's testimony revealed and the identification to Roger Nunez should have been the key element in the investigation.

However, the detectives didn't look further into the matter or try to locate Nunez. They filed a formal report on August 30, effectively concluding the case. It is no secret that the NOPD has been criticised from the beginning and through the years for the way they handled the case. Then Delery Edwards insists that, unfortunately, this criticism is well-deserved.

He found the language used in the records to be unnatural. Some times, they were even offensive, as they interrogated witnesses about their sexual life and not the particular case in hand. OPD detectives at this year's 40th anniversary, told that time magazine. There are plenty of instances when you'll feel like you're an investigator know what transpired and who was responsible however legally, you're not able to snare the person.

It's just a matter of time. I'm sure. I am certain in my heart it is this guy who started the fire. Evidently, footprints left on the fluid lighter container or witnesses to witness him fleeing from the building would have provided more reliable evidence, however, they had enough evidence to locate Roger Nunez and bring him into the investigation. Given the information we have about Roger in the future, there is an excellent chance that he'd have admitted guilt or covered into the flames.

Marshall investigators were more thorough. They interviewed witnesses with the same questions and many more. Their reporting and language did not seem difficult. They also spoke to their witnesses in the slang employed. Contrary to the police who cleaned them, when they interrogated Roger Nunez, he claimed that he suffered the broken tooth from 3 black males in Iberville who took his wallet, and then dragged him down prior to the fire.

He acknowledged going to the upper level on during the time that the fire started, however he denied inflicting troubles or getting thrown out. The investigators also discovered an entry in Nunez hospital records that said that the hospital's administration called the NOPD to inform them that Nunez was being discharged but nobody showed up or was it the chief who was there.

She spoke with Scarborough first, and then told the police to collect his statements to the medical facility. The police were way ahead police in every step , and showed more interest in investigating leads. Roger Nunez was 26 years old at the time of the fire. His parents divorced, and he came from small town in rural Louisiana as well as Vermilion Parish within Southwestern Louisiana.

The area was extremely impoverished area , with many people earning their living from fishing for oysters or shrimps and working at oil drilling rigs. The area was also highly Catholic area. A gay young man or a woman could have been uneasy there and not suitable for the work workforce. He moved to New Orleans in the year 1970. He worked as a nurse's aid, and also as a janitorial worker.

He worked as a bartender at Jean Davis's Bar. When he was involved in the fire Nunez was convicted of minor infractions. His acquaintance claimed that in the seventies, he was hustler. The hideaway wasn't a gay bar however, it was a welcoming place to hustlers who had gene Davis who was the owner. The bar was often a place where they would sleep at the beginning of afternoon after the fire.

This was seen going into the hideaway along with an older man. they sat drinking until another young male joined them. The man occurred to be Alan , Alan the first person to inform police towards the house of Nina's Godrey and was also known as a hustler. In the evening after the fire was able to get Nunez his elder John out of his grasp.

They were gone for a time. Gene Davis claimed the fact that Roger Nunez was visibly upset due to this, and was drinking heavily Godrey. The older man came back at about 5:00 pm and had a drink with Roger however it was evident that the man was furious. The man from the past gave Roger $20 in an attempt to make things more palatable. Davis told him that Roger suggested.

Three men go upstairs to get an alcohol bust Davis says that he then intervened and advised the man who was older not to go, as he was drunk to walk up the stairs. He also taken him to the hospital after the bar patron fell off a stool. Roger left to go to the beer bust. Alan Godrey along with the elderly man went off on their own about two hours and half later. Alan returned and headed to the upstairs area, leaving about seven twenty.

He denied that he saw Roger be punched, but later admitted to having seen the bar owner kick him out. the bar's owner and his friend. Gene Davis was a cagey witness. He was convicted of child pornography, as well as sexual relations with a teenager that we consider rape today, even though. The charges weren't made that way in the past.

The point is that the fact that he was not a good citizen, and he was in an encounter with the police. He likely knew more than he was passing go concerning Roger Nunez and the fire Davis was put through an evaluation of stress which was utilized as an alternative to an interview. The technician claimed that he was not answering a few vital questions about Roger as well as the fire.

The test cannot be used in court, however it's important to note, however, he did identify Roger Nunez as the man who was involved in the battle and the one he to throw out as well as the one he was trying to present to an officer following the fire. Roger Nunez took the same test, and the stress suggested it was a lie. If he didn't answer this question: did you actually start the fire in the lounge upstairs?

He was even advised by his lawyer not to take the exam around halfway through. It's safest to say it was not a good look. This was also not legally admissible in court. However, it's a good interrogation tool. But without witnesses or evidence the police did not have sufficient evidence to warrant their take the necessary steps to. Yes. However, the arson investigator stuck on this Nunez theory and continued to interview his associates and friends.

Roger Nunez met a woman called Elaine in the early part of 1974. He got married to her in the spring of 1974, she was 49, and the man was 27. This was thought to be an unplanned marriage. The seizures were getting more severe. He underwent surgery the was done the same year to remove a tumor in his brain shortly after their wedding. He admitted to her that his sexual orientation, but they decided to remain in a separate way.

He was in a trailer that was located in her backyard lane. She went out on the morning of November 15th 1974 and came across Roger Nunez dead. He had ingested 3 prescription pills, along with a six-pack of beers. There was no note left however, based on the amount of the amount of medication was found in his system, and the beers, his demise was declared a suicide.

One of Roger's close friends named Ralph was extremely angry after he heard about the incident and decided to go to for a drink, post office, Phyllis Steve's brand new bar. Phil saw the man crying and asked him to explain what was going on. Ralph was shocked when Ralph explained, Michael Scarborough, who was in the bar, laughed which made everyone uncomfortable.

Then he added, it was the one who caused the fire to the lounge upstairs. You know, now Phil started questioning Ralph. And he confessed the fact that Roger Nunez had confessed to him that he had been drinking. He was the one who started the fire. Phil immediately contacted an arson investigation team. Then Ralph was brought in to provide an explanation.

He claimed it was because Roger Nunez had told him several times that he set the fire in the upstairs room because he was furious for being kicked out. He even informed him that he purchased the lighter fluid from Walgreens at the corner. Ralph repeated his claim that Roger had always been drunk whenever he shared the story . He also said that he would return the next day. Once he was sober. Roger Nunez also befriended a sister, a nun, and Mary Steven.

Although she didn't mention that the truth however, he did confess to her that the possibility of being a suspect. She was of the opinion that it was a way to appear more masculine since, quote, it was to the stage where he could not accept who was. The arson investigators continued to talk to family and friends about Roger Nunez after his death.

In August of 1975, the group submitted their case before the new Orleans da. They had hoped that it could be enough to allow the da to declare a definitive closure of the case. However, it did not happen. It was a long time before there was end to the story for those in the LGBT community. The police fought for years to continue investigating the case and speak to a witness who claimed to be sister Mary Stevenson.

She had a relationship with a gay man who confessed, and later took his own life. Another person came forward. Miss Fury, a drag queen Miss Fury had seen Roger Nunez and she told Johnny Townsend that Roger had confessed to her when intoxicated. It was Christmas Eve following the fire. He wept, she said, and shared a quote with her.

He was only trying to create an ember to ignite in the smoke. He only wanted to scare everyone. He wasn't aware that the entire area would burst into fires. It appears to be Roger Nunez, his conscience was killing him while the time he was drunk. He was repeatedly convicted by acquaintances and finally took his own life and was devastated.

Troy Perry said on the documentary in the upstairs of FIRNA the quote that if Perry was the one who caused the fire, he would have been the 33rd person who died in the fire. Perry insisted that he forgives Nunez and that is the feeling of many, however no one who had endured any hardship, so he was not aiming to cause an unimaginable massacre.

Remember when the Walgreens clerk who insisted that he requested the smallest bottle? Regina Adam said on the same documentary quote: I don't believe he was aware of the implications. The number of people he could harm or how many lives he could impact. The author Johnny Townson was also interviewed in the documentary and stated that gay people could have been healed faster.

If they'd felt there was a plan to resolve the issue. Today, people are aware about the dog who was a part of arson investigators, but since it was not widely known at the time, and people were angry and hurt. In fact, for a lengthy time, the investigation was eventually closed in the year 1980. The report basically stated that the sole suspect committed suicide. The report also quoted.

The investigators were 100% satisfied that it was him who caused the fire. the civil lawsuits were a bit tangled, as to who was responsible. The building's owner Philistine, the City as well as the fire Marshall as well as the combined lawsuits filed by victims and survivors. Families were awarded $28 million. nearly two decades after the fire. A civil district judge found that the plaintiffs didn't have any legal cause to bring a lawsuit for damages against city.

Phil Steve eventually went bankrupt fighting lawsuits. In the end after nearly 4 years of court disputes many of the lawsuits were dismissed. The sole person legally responsible was the one who ignited the fire. There was no negligence by the part of any other agency or individual can be established. Phyllis Steve died in 2007 however, he refuses to talk to reporters or to speak in public about the fire up to the present.

He relocated into Arkansas with his partner and was quoted by time magazine that on the 40th anniversary of the event that, as history is written it's best to leave this chapter out. Clayton Delery Edwards takes on the history of the fire in the upstairs lounge within his memoir, since the fire is an issue that has been the subject of heated debate about whether or whether the fire upstairs set off the gay rights movement in New Orleans. Orleans historians, pointing at the event and the subsequent protest by Anita Bryant in 1977.

She was a deeply Christian performer who spoke out against classrooms and homosexuals and was often quoted as saying that since homosexuals were unable to reproduce. They're forced to hire. She was a hit with a couple of records in the 50s and sixties. However, at the end of the seventies she was watching, and then turned to the political arena.

She and her husband advocated against an ordinance adopted in her home town that is located in Dade County, Florida. It's illegal to discriminate in employment due to sexual orientation. Bryant was successful in June of 1977 , and was encouraged to continue her anti-gay cause. Bryant was actually booked to perform in the city of new Orleans.

Before she made her debut in the spotlight in the nation. A homophobic bigot she was scheduled to perform at a series of pop concerts at the brand new Orleans city auditorium. On June 17, and the following day, her supporters staged a protest before the newspaper and ad hoc support prior to the performance. Also, the NOPD has promised her security.

The gay rights protest in the community was well-organized by two groups: that of the Gertrude Stein society and human equal rights for all. They also held their own demonstration. Then, over 200 protesters stood outside the auditorium during the show, wearing signs and shirt. The protest was peaceful but the images are quite powerful.

There were some boos in the crowd for the performance of Brian, however it was not all that disruptive. However, by the time Saturday arrived the protesters had swelled to 1500 people , and Bryant supporters were part of a small group that was less than forty. The gay protesters started with a march at Jackson Square, and then walked throughout the French quarter, before heading to the auditorium and shouting.

Oh, Hey ho. Anita Bryant has got to leave. It was a quiet protest but it was more louder. Anita Bryant gave an interview to the Times Picayune and then later in what she saidwas, I'd rather see my child dead than gay. It is clear it was Anita Bryant's protest Anita Bryant protest galvanized the gay community and their friends however like Delery Edwards points out in his book The upstairs lounge, arson, and the seeds were planted in the upstairs lounge.

The main event was the large turnout to the main Memorial service. The mourners who decided to go to the front of the church and stand in front of the cameras. gay people as well as their allies had taken the first ever stand in the church that day. In the weeks following an incident, the gay-friendly coalition was created in response to the fire . It also declared the opening of an aerial health clinic in the area of North Rampart.

The clinic was established to provide an enclave for gay patients to seek treatment for syphilis and gonorrhea, not having to worry about being exposed or being treated by uncaring doctors. It was established before the finding about HIV as well as it's AIDS epidemic. Six weeks later, after the fire, in hopes of resolving the mayor's moon, Landro met with the GPC and appointed gay and lesbians for his committee of human relationships.

In September , following the fire, journalist Joan Treadway wrote a six parts series on homosexuality in the times, Picayune , the series of stories. Although at the time, it was a bit deaf tone was quite novel as the first time anyone wrote about the gay community in which people were able to share their experiences and efforts to overcome homophobia and ignorance and homophobia. Delery Edwards was and Townsend's novels as well as documentaries like upstairs Inferno.

Additionally, you should mention the huge campaign to raise money, the assistance of survivors as well as to assist in the burial of the dead. It was the Reverend Troy Perry had been characterized as a fairy carpetbagger. He was tired, Leslie, in this campaign, along with the other members of the MCC ministry, and LGBT activists. The campaign brought in $18,000. Clayton Delery Edwards notes that most of the donations came from individuals. $5 here or $10 there.

For the first time , the homosexual community banded together in order to aid one another during a time of immense need. This was the precursor to the concerted activism that is expected to be a part of this AIDS crisis. In the aftermath, the gay community came back, it was united. There had been more than 26,000 deaths from AIDS prior to the time that president Ronald Reagan would even publicly admit to the epidemic. Both events, the fire in the upstairs as well as that Anita Bryant protest were watershed occasions to promote gay pride.

It's probably fair to say that the fire opened the door wide and the Bryant protests destroyed it. It's not hard to understand why people are so strongly opposed to the incident in 1991. The Louisiana state museum was able to run it once more. The exhibit was titled the devouring element, which was dedicated to the recent Orleans historical fires. The museum did not include the upstairs lounge that is, in reality the most deadly fire in New Orleans history.

After much anger, they released an unsigned statement regarding finding enough photographs or stories to include. The fire was difficult to investigate Clayton Delery Edwards pointed out that they were not having any trouble getting archive footage fires that occurred in the 18th century, close to 20 years later, the lounge upstairs was ablaze that claimed 32 lives and many survivors were neglected.

However, public opinion did shift in the 30th anniversary year. The year 2003 saw the bronze monument was put up on the sidewalk in front of the Iberville street's entry point. It contains the names of all those who were deceased. In 2012, the mayor Mitch Landrow, son of moon, Landrow introduced sweeping reforms to deal with human rights violations in the areas of domestic violence, sexual assault and lastly the way that police personnel interact with gay, lesbian and transgendered individuals during the 40th anniversary of the fire in 2013. A production called upstairs premiere the city of Orleans about the fire.

The documentary and the lounge upstairs was the first to premiere and a number of other things. Newspapers and articles were put out in celebration of the fire's author, Clayton Delery Edwards and artists. Schuyler Fein addressed an audience of more than 200 at the famous newly opened Orleans collection, which is a privately owned museum. The an annual New Orleans jazz funerals. Orleans funeral procession that went from the main entrance of the museum, through the French quarter, and then to the front door of the old upstairs lounge.

City Mayor Mitch Landrow issued a city proclamation acknowledging the tragedy. archbishop Gregory Aymond apologized on behalf of the diocese for not taking action during the fire. Every year, there is an annual Memorial funeral in jazz on June 24 on the second floor and the structure on Iberville and Charters, that was the place where the upstairs used to be, never was used as a bar.

It's now storage space, and the flip houses are over it. Sit empty. It is crucial to remember that the massacre in the upstairs lounge was not the result of a hate crime, but. The public often sees it in this way. Roger Nunez made a terrible uninformed and drunken choice that claimed the lives of many even his own. One could argue that his own homophobia and hatred of himself caused the tragedy, but it wasn't really an attack on gays.

This to me makes it even more tragic. A gay man who was trying to figure out his own identity made a terrible mistake, however the loss of 32 souls in the flames were not without cause. This lounge upstairs has earned its place in the history of. While it might not be a brand new Orleans Stonewall however, it's not less significant to the LGBTQ community.

The upstairs was the place where people always felt at ease The place where everyone could be at ease. Today, pride is celebrated with fervor and loudly in new Orleans, not just at Southern lavishness, but all over the world. you're unable to throw a stone without hitting an open gay bar within the refrigerator quarter. Personally, these are my personal favorite types of love.

Chapter 3: Deathbed Confession At Sycamore

Seven-year old Maria Rudolph was excited about winter. She was eager to see the first snowfalls which would befall her this year. On the 3rd day of December 1957, she left the safety of her home in order to spend time with her favorite friend Kathy Sigman. The incident that occurred on that day stunned all the residents of Sycamore, Illinois. The girl's disappearance was unlike anything they'd before witnessed previously in Sycamore, Illinois. The night was full of snowflakes. It was dark and cold. Maria was then begging her mom if she would like to leave their home to play with her friend Kathy. The parents were unaware that the dark shadowy figure stood outside their house to kidnap their daughters.

On the 12th of March 1952 Maria Rudolph was born to her parents, Michael and Frances Ivy Rudolph. Maria was a huge fan of playing and spent a lot of time outdoors in her mother's garden. In the second grade, she was introduced to and became acquainted with Kathy Sigman, also a neighbor. When it started with snow falling, Maria approached her mother and asked permission to go outside to spend time with her friend Kathy. Due to the conditions Maria's mother was not convinced about her daughter playing with her in snow. After much begging several minutes, Maria's mom let her take a snowy walk.

Maria got out of the front door and ran toward Kathy's house. She pleaded with Kathy's parents to allow her to be with them. However, Maria grabbed Kathy and took her to the road, where they would play "Duck the car" with the snow.

While playing on the street they spotted an automobile coming towards them. When it stopped in front of them, a child aged around 18 years old arrived and offered for a play date with them. He walked up to them and identified himself as Johnny and then said he would play them by taking them on an excursion on a piggyback. Maria took the offer however, Kathy did not. In a pleasant manner he asked his girls whether they enjoyed playing with dolls. In a rousing manner, Maria proclaimed her love for dolls. After that, she rushed home to get her favourite doll to show him the one she had only met only a couple of minutes ago.

After Maria was back from getting her doll, she walked up to Johnny and Kathy immediately after she left them. Just after a couple of minutes she was playing with Johnny as well as Kathy; Kathy began to beg about the cold, and ran back to her home, where she quickly grabbed her gloves that protected their hands from brutal cold. In a matter of seconds, Kathy ran out of her home to continue her playing alongside Johnny along with Maria.

Surprisingly the moment Kathy arrived at the location at which she had was with Johnny and Maria taking piggyback rides but she was unable to locate her companions, and she was unable to locate Johnny. Kathy was screaming Maria's name loudly several times, but could see no trace for her friend Maria. In that moment, Kathy got confused and thought about whether Maria was hiding from Kathy who was looking for her. She returned to her house and scoured the garden to determine whether Maria played hide-and-seek. But, Kathy saw no sign of her beloved friend. things got out of control, so Kathy decided to call Maria's home. Maria's older brother Chuck aged eleven years old, responded to the constant knocking at the door and informed Kathy that Maria might be hiding in the garden, hiding. This led Kathy go through the garden as well as the other gardens of neighbors, but found no trace of Maria. Then she returned to the house of Maria and knocked.

In anger, Chuck opened the door and began to join Kathy looking for Maria within a couple of minutes shortly after Kathy was knocked. After a few hours, the hunt for Maria was intensified and Chuck decided to inform his parents. The parents began the search for Maria shortly after Maria's disappearance. Maria The family then took the decision to call the police. From the moment they were involved, the search for Maria within the neighborhood started. Residents armed with rifles machetes, sticks pistols, handguns and other weapons took to the streets and knocked on doors with proper search warrants issued to the authorities. The Lieutenant Patrick Soler led the investigation and placed numerous roadblocks on roads that were rural. The Lieutenant allowed citizens the ability to search each trunk of their cars. After a few days, the police were able to search every trunk. by before the citizens took matters in their own hands however, after a thorough searching, Maria was no where to be located. After extensive investigation, several witnesses have confirmed the fact that they heard children screaming at 7 pm the night Maria disappeared. Police located the doll Maria was rushing home to find Johnny close to a fence however Maria Rudolph was still nowhere to be located.

The police suspected the case to be kidnapping , and they believed Maria's abductor crossed across states, requiring the Federal Government's aid. It was the Federal Government put together an precise timeline that included the time Maria was missing that was between 6:45 pm between 7:00 pm and 6:45 pm. Additionally the screams that witnesses heard on the day that she disappeared been in line with the time of her disappearance that was compiled by the Federal Government.

In the wake of Maria disappearing, children were not playing with Kathy as parents feared that their children would disappear. The police had to put Kathy to protective custody since they believed that the kidnapper was likely to return to complete the work he begun. The police also tried to make Kathy Sigman recall the image of her closest friend's abductor using images of ex-offenders that were believed to be involved in having committed the same crime. One of the images that was identified by Kathy as Johnny was of a man who was used by the police to identify the other suspects. Unfortunately this guy Kathy recognized was in jail at the time Maria was abducted. Kathy was constantly under pressure when she was handed an endless array of possible images compiled from the department of police. The person Kathy has identified as Johnny was the result of a lengthy interrogation by the police about the eight-year-old girl who had recently lost her best friend. The general description Kathy provided to police regarding Johnny was young , in his 20s. He was blonde with a blond hair. He additionally had a slim, chin with an opening between his teeth.

A couple of weeks had passed by and the case was growing and caused ripples across the nation that led the president of the day at the time and President Eisenhower along with J Edgar Hoover to take an interest. The search for the missing woman grew more intense over time, but not a complete loss, and not until five months, on April 26th of 1958, two miles to the east in Woodbine Illinois, the decomposed body of a girl was discovered beneath the branches of a fallen tree. It was later confirmed as the corpse of Maria Rudolph. When she was found , she was wearing an undershirt and a shirt that had socks on the feet. The police investigation, with the aid of forensic experts, could not determine the reason for her death. In the following days, James Furlong a coroner who assisted in the investigation of bodies at the scene of the crime made an order to not allow any photos of the body would be taken, due to concerns about the possibility of the photos being published to the press regardless of how crucial it may be to FBI investigators.

The murder was deemed unsolved because the perpetrator could not have been held responsible. However, prior to the time that the case was shut down by police detectives over the years the man identified as John Tessier was investigated in the same town a few days following the kidnapping of Maria Ridulph. John's parents gave police with an explanation in the same evening Maria had been declared missing. John Tessier's parents informed the police that John had taken the trip in Rockford, Illinois; at the date, John was enlisted in the Armed Forces before which he was tested for polygraphs and was able to pass the test.

The detectives accepted the evidence John's parents had given to police officers, which led the police to remove his name from the list of suspects in Maria's murder. The police were also convinced due to the fact that Tessiers family members provided the searchers of Maria's remains with flashlights on the night that she disappeared.

Months and days passed following Maria was laid to rest. The sorrow of this tragic loss remained inside the Ridulphs and Kathy Sigman's loved ones each day. As time passed the families of both families ceased to be the focus of attention of the general public. In the end, as some time had gone by, the public started to forget about the death of Maria. It was a decade since the deathbed confession was released to reopen the case which was closed.

In 1994, the mom of John Tessier, who was believed to be the murderer confessed at her deathbed. This led to the police reopening the investigation. John's mom on her deathbed informed Janet Tessier- her daughter who was her daughter, that she wouldn't be capable of leaving this world with a secret within her heart for this long. Her mother explained to Janet that the two girls were playing ago, and when one went missing and the other was brutally injured, John did it, and she was required to tell the person immediately.

In the wake of this devastating confession, Janet Tessier couldn't take this information given to her for granted. Janet began to realize that there was truth to what her mother had said to her since all of her siblings were raised knowing that their mother was always there to protect John from consequences for his behavior. Jean Tessier, who was also the sister of John and Janet said to CBS the news that they'd heard their mom told the police a false confession while the investigation was on. The police resisted the confession on deathbed because John was exempted in the listing of suspects in 1958. This led to Maria's Maria murder case closed for 10 years.

In August 2004 Janet made the decision to reach out for help from police officials from Illinois State police department. The police began questioning all members of the Tessier family, and shocking revelations began to surface. John's younger sister informed investigators that John had been abusing sexually her for many years, and this was not a normal conduct he was taught by his father. It was something that the family was aware of, but couldn't stop. The suspicions grew as police decided to find an eyewitness to help identify John Tessier out of a list of suspects. Detectives compiled photos of men in their teens who were suspected back in 1950, to determine whether Kathy Sigman could recognize her friend's kidnapper.

Luckily, Kathy Sigman picked John Tessier photo from the group to coincide with Maria's kidnapper. However, after further investigation, John Tessier was nowhere to be seen in Illinois. Detectives were able to discover that John was living in Washington under the name of Jack McCullough. John was married to a woman and also had a step-daughter who were both shocked by the information the police had against John. When John was asked regarding Maria she was, he told police Maria was a good girl. Maria was loved by the community and was a lovely girl who was beautiful and had brown eyes and hair. John wouldn't think of abducting her. His response raised suspicions about John was the kidnapper due to the amount of all the details he shared about Maria. It also appeared as if that he was in love with her, and he attempted to defend himself against any question he was asked. For instance, the police were able to question McCullough about his conduct with his sister's sexuality and he resisted the question but later admitted it was an sex game with her, but he never considered it the abuse.

Jack McCullough's interrogations triggered so many suspicions. This later led to him being arrested for murder and kidnapping, 54 years after Maria Ridulph's passing. After McCullough was convicted of murder, other young girls began coming forward about sexual assault experiences they experienced with Jack. McCullough was an officer in the police force back during the 80s. The incident led him to take advantage of girls who were young and abuse them sexually which led to him losing his position as an officer in the police force.

The entire the state of Illinois and Washington identified John Tessier later known as Jack McCullough as a murderer or pedophile, an agressor, kidnapper and a sexual offender. The state was determined to get John Tessier to be put away for good, but there was no evidence to prove he was being the killer of Maria Ridulph and he was subsequently accused of rape and sexual assault on his younger sister. The state did not have any reliable evidence to link McCullough to, and they were forced to analyze and exhume Maria Rudolph's remains and discovered new evidence regarding the reason for her death, like evidence on her collarbone that revealed that she was strangled to death.

The police did not find any DNA evidence, no fingerprints, and no physical evidence to put to prove the case of John Tessier. The public was left to question whether that he was actually the killer. The public was convinced that John Tessier to be the murderer, but they had no proof against his claims. There were numerous criticisms from people who were against the lineup put out by police on Maria's murder, since John Tessier's image stood out without doubt. Many also believed in the claims of his sister as well as the evidence that John changed his address with a different name and as if he had fled from the whole thing. This impacted him later in life, but he managed to get past the allegations through luck.

In the year John Tessier had enrolled for the Armed Forces, a report from the DeKalb County State gave evidence of a phone call that showed that McCollough was in Rockford about 40 miles to the northwest of Sycamore to sign up for in the Armed Forces at the time of the kidnapping. The evidence proved that it was impossible to McCollough to have abducted Maria and then returned to Rockford just in time to make a telephone call. Additionally, DeKalb County State's Attorney Richard Schmack spoke about the conviction of John Tessier and further fought the decision to keep him in jail because it was not a great reputation for the community or a fitting tribute to Maria Ridulph.

In April of 2016, McCollough was ordered to be released. Following that, DeKalb County

Associate Judge William Brady granted Jack a certificate of innocence.

Chapter 4: Horror Across Wheaton Mall

John Lyon met Mary at Xavier University Cincinnati. They never had any thought of marrying because they were students at the university. Mary was originally from Erlanger, Kentucky, while John was born and raised in Chicago. In the following years they got married in Erlanger and had the first of their children, Jay. After John completed his studies from high school, he sought a job with the broadcasting station located in Ohio and was offered the job at the time Sheila was born. Then, the couple moved to Illinois and was offered an opportunity to work as an announcer on radio. A short time after, Catherine was born, and John was able to work at an NBC and radio station. A couple of years had passed byand the couple welcomed their first baby, Joe. John and Mary played banjo and guitar in a folk ensemble. They were an extremely cute couple and had a great and enjoyable time.

The 1970s were the time that John became a radio presenter at WMAL which was one of Washington's most well-known radio stations in DC. John was a skilled radio announcer and his work resulted in a steady increase in his earnings. He also served as disc jockey fill-in He was a great dancer and had a humorous personality.

On the 29th of March, 1975 in the suburbs of Washington DC, it was cold and hot the day that Catherine 10, who was then 10 and Sheila twelve years old were at school for their spring break. John had been working on a night shift, and then drove home the day prior to. He arrived home at 6:45 am the next morning. Tired and exhausted, he went to bed to relax after showering. Sheila and Catherine wanted to give their dad money, so they gave him two dollars. Following that, the kids decided to go to Wheaton Mall to purchase two pizza slices. The older Sheila did not like having time spent with her young sister, but lately Sheila was being seen with her little sister, Catherine

In the afternoon, John woke up from his long nap to find an empty home. The boys had gone out to play with their neighbour while Mary went bowling with her friend Brenda. After a while, Mary came home with their son Joe shortly after John was awake from his sleep. The next night, Mary took to cleaning up their backyard. Immediately after she had cleaned up her work she started to get anxious over her children. Typically, both girls were up early to dinner every night. Sheila always called her brothers to stay home for dinner, even when they were playing with their neighbors playing. However, on this particular day, she saw no signs of her daughters. Sheila did not make a phone call at her siblings. The family was eating dinner and the girls didn't show to return in their homes. The incident occurred in 1975. evidently, abduction was the last thing one might be thinking of at the time. There was still no indication of the girls' disappearance the family waited, and after having completed dinner. Mary began to call all her neighbors and acquaintances and everyone she spoke to did not see any sign of the girls.

After that, the family drove around searching for the girls. Hours passed by without any girls' presence. The family started to feel guilty over their girls as the time was passing. Then, John decided to call police to complain about his daughters' disappearance. The police were involved in the search for the girls, and they realized that they were dealing with a different issue completely. John and Mary confessed to police that they were always respectful and adhered to the rules. Catherine had an athletic personality and was a funny girl. Sheila was to the contrary was reserved and shy. Sheila had just started helping her mother with house chores, and also babysitting the little baby, and also assisted their mother with cooking. Sheila was a student at Newport Junior High, and she was in the seventh grade. She was planning to join the cheerleading squad at the school. The police inspected and searched the girl's home and found that nothing was missing from their rooms. The girls' clothes were in good condition and their piggybanks remained unopened.

John felt that his daughters did not have any intention of leaving the home. After having seen all the fragments of evidence, John was wishing they had been alive and wished they'd run away.

The majority of cases of missing children seemed to be solved within the first 24 hours after their disappearance. In those thousands reported missing child instances, only a few hundred have been reported to have been kidnapped by strangers. In this instance two girls were missing and were found dead at the same time in a rare event. Additionally, research has revealed that families are the most likely to commit crimes against children, however this was a unique case as Lyon's family was believed to be a beautiful and happy family. Sheila always wore her bulky glasses and blonde pigtails that was cute. Kate was a teen and had shorter blonde hair and freckled eyes. They both have drawings about their families that were pasted in their rooms. Indeed they appeared to be adorable children. While it was an stressful situation for police, as they could read the drawings on their walls but it was an incident which the police could understand since they had children similar like Kathy as well as Sheila.

The terrible situation resulted in Mary put under the care of a doctor who prescribed tranquilizers. John was left with no choice but to control his emotions. He was never calm at moments. However, the couple was determined to find their daughters, and were prepared to do whatever was necessary to return them to their homes. John and Mary were still hopeful that their daughter would return home within a couple of days of misunderstanding.

The Lyon family resided in Kennington near the north of Washington and during the 1970s, Kennington was a bedroom neighborhood mostly intended for Washington commuters. Along with the nearby town that was Wheaton, Kennington was home for many successful couples searching for a secure place to raise their families.

As time passed the media picked up on the news of the disappearance of the girls and, in the following days over 300 people contacted police for tips and details regarding the missing girls. The police department in the area searched the woods, and found empty houses and sewer drivers were sent to investigate. The police interviewed all workers and residents but nobody could provide any concrete evidence. It appeared as if the girls were disappearing out of thin air.

After the girl's disappearance reported missing on April 1 the 18-year-old Lloyd Welch went to Wheaton Plaza and resisted his grandmother's instructions to him not to be involved in the investigation. Lloyd did not stop there because he believed that he had information to provide to police, and no one was aware of his motives. Lloyd was a scrawny person with long dark hair that parted in the middle. He always wore a headband , and was a dropout of seventh grade. Lloyds family was known for its history of incestuous lies and numerous reported petty crimes. This was not a good thing for him when he was a child.

Wheaton Plaza Wheaton Plaza is a shopping mall with a few small specialty shops. It was home to the Montgomery Ward department as well as the movie theater, which included fast-food restaurants. The incident occurred during spring break, and usually the plaza was packed with children who were trying to keep themselves entertained, just as Sheila as well as Kathy. Lloyd confessed to that the Wheaton mall security guards that he knew of missing girl. Then , he was transferred by the department of police where he made a written statement. Lloyd was not truthful. He claimed that he was at the mall on March 29th along with Helen, his spouse. Helen. Lloyd admitted to the police that the age was 22. He also told police that he had seen two young girls who matched that Lyon sisters' descriptions. They were speaking with a man who was holding the tape recorder. The moment he spoke, everything the information he provided was a lie since the police identified the man who was carrying the tape recorder identified as a primary suspect. Lloyd stated that the tape recorder's man as being dressed in a jacket, and carrying the briefcase.

Lloyd heard the man tell his daughters that he had recorded voices. The story of the tape recorder's man became an extremely popular story for police and community about missing people Therefore, it did not contribute for the police investigation. The tape recorder man also stated that he observed the girls talk with the tape recording for between five and 10 minutes. This was a very suspect report since there was no reason for why he been watching the girls for this long period of time. Others told police that a man appeared to be Lloyd was looking at them in the mall. Lloyd also was a bit naive in the information that he provided to police. He claimed to have witnessed the man enter a vehicle with the girls. He claimed that the car had a scratch on the rare right side with a broken tail light. Lloyd also stated that the car was equipped with an white Maryland plate in its rear.

Many people believe that the more information given on a case the more trustworthy the information could be. Lloyd also was willing to take an examination for polygraphs, which did not pass following the test. Lloyd was later able to admit in front of the officers that all of the details he shared about the girls as well as the tape recorder was not accurate, and this led to the police dismiss Lloyd for revealing the wrong details to receive the reward money to see if they can find the Lyon sisters' kidnapper. The mistake that the police did not make was in locking Lloyd in a solitary cell as an suspect. He was able to provide a lot of information about the investigation, however the police viewed him as drunk and incompetent. Lloyd's interview with police turned out as a transcript of six pages but it was later discarded and discarded over the course of 38 years.

The case was revisited in 2013. While the police did not find the sketch description of an eyewitness at the time the sketch description appeared to be in line with Lloyd's appearance the day that the girls disappeared. Danette was the name of the girl that portrayed the sketched suspect to police officers, and she was only an eon more advanced than Sheila. She claimed that she was pursued by a man on the same day and that he was seen looking at her and her friends. The man was young and of late teens. He was 5-11 or 6 feet tall. He carried a moustache.

In 2013, Detective Chris Hamrock found a file regarding Lloyd Welch's confession to police in 1975. The statement was later dismissed by was dismissed by the police as being false. After Lloyd's testimony to police, Chris Hamrock found that the person Lloyd provided to police was walking with an leg. This led Chris look up Lloyd for years to discover the fact that Lloyd was in prison for a time, serving an inmate of the state over 33 years. Additionally, Lloyd was found guilty of molesting a child as young as 10.

On the 16th of October 13 in 2013 on October 16, 2013, On the 16th of October, 2013, Detective Chris Hamrock and Dave Davis traveled with Montgomery deputy States Attorney Pete Fenney to Delaware to talk to Lloyd. When they arrived, the first answer Lloyd gave the detectives was alarming. He explained that he was aware of the reason they came to meet him due to the two girls who were missing. It was nearly forty years after the disappearances of the two girls. Lloyd had been convicted of numerous crimes that included the crime of burglary, drunk driving and the robbery. His previous history of sexual assault with small girls made detectives wonder whether he was involved to the girls who disappeared. Police had made an extensive list of suspects in connection with the disappearance, one of them being Ray Moleski, but died in prison in the year 2005. Ray was thought to be to be a pedophile. In 1975 in 1975, he contacted the police and advised that they should grant protection to the kidnapper when he handed over the girl back to the family. After offering his offer to police in the following year after, he killed his wife and child at his home and was later taken into custody. While in prison Ray admitted to his fellow prisoners that he knew the location where the body of the girls was. He said that the body was located in the basement of his house The police searched, but did not find anything. Following Ray was charged with murdering his son and wife and daughter, the police uncovered that he murdered them in order to keep his identity from being exposed in the Lyon sisters murder. In the night Ray was imprisoned and he was found with the phone numbers of Lyon written on the paper of his father; evidently, Ray had a connection to the investigation. Why did Ray call Lloyd's number on the day that the girls disappeared. Witnesses reported seeing an individual with the same description as Ray in Wheaton Plaza on the day the girls left He was noticed taking girls and boys from a car to have sexual activity.

Investigator Chris Hamrock searched for solid evidence but in vain; he came across Lloyd's confession in 1975, in which Lloyd stated that the person who took the girls walked on an limb. This information was enough to get Chris exuberant. When detective Chris obtained the mugshot of Lloyd that was taken in the year 1975, it was in line with the sketch picture Danette handed to police that day in the case of Lyon sisters disappearance. Although time has passed, Lloyd now had a gray beard and a grey goatee. It was amazing what he resembled in the sketch. This led to Lloyd an obvious suspect. The police believed

Lloyd was working along with Ray to lure girls out of the mall. Additionally, the police believed that a girl of a certain age would be more bonded to a boy in his teens than men in their twenties or perhaps Sheila and Kate were aware of Lloyd as a friend.

The FBI was able to assist the police establish a timeline in connection with the disappearance of the girl. Lloyd was involved in the carnival and was able to frequent travel. The police investigated Lloyd's journey to cases of missing girls across the globe and discovered something odd. The police officer had a meeting with Lloyd for interrogation in October of 2013; during the interrogation, Lloyd kept making noises about how he was resentful of his prison experience along with how his father messed his life when he was young and didn't know his mother. Lloyd was aged 56 in the moment of interrogation, and stated that he felt the need to make changes since he discovered God inside prison, and felt the need to serve his fellow citizens. Though he stated that he was not an child mole, he was found to have beat the daughter of his girlfriend because the girl was drunk. While he claimed that the laws of Delaware were too loose and unjust, he was sorry for the act and that the daughter of his girlfriend was supposed to be his step-daughter. Detective Davis was forced to sit and take in the conversation and nod his head for long periods of time. The interrogation video of the interview showed the detective Davis was establishing a pleasant connection and Lloyd; Davis also ordered food for Lloyd.

The detectives stopped from questioning and held an informal meeting in a separate room. After the break when detective Davis took a photo of Ray Moleski. He presented the picture to Lloyd. Lloyd was able to recognize Moleski and he told him that he had seen Moleski was riding in the road in a Plymouth station wagon. He would often give Moleski rides to his home, but they did not talk much. Lloyd attempted to establish an impression of familiarity, and removed him from Moleski. Detective David spoke to Lloyd about how he was involved himself in the investigation back in 1975. He also inquired of Lloyd why the police didn't take his case seriously. Lloyd added that he was miles from Wheaton Plaza on the time when the girls disappeared. He observed a man in black clothing enter an automobile, placing two girls on the rear of the car after which the vehicle sped away. When inquired about the statement from the police which he made, he explained that he never went to the police station, but called the police via the payphone. In response, Lloyd was asked why he had given an entirely different account from 1975, he explained that he was planning to be transferred to a Maryland jail and that he would cease giving information until he was successfully transferred. Why would he want to compel police officers to cease talking even though he'd already given many details. When Lloyd was presented with his declaration on the subject in 1995, he stated that it was not his memory of visiting the police station and having the polygraph test.

In this particular moment, police were attempting to obtain an official confess from Lloyd. But he eventually reverted to his story of having seen the girls walking down the street with Moleski but not in the mall. Detective David advised Lloyd that he was not an suspect, but might be in the event that he continued to provide false details. While Davis believed Lloyd had lied about details and was convinced that he was involved in helping Moleski kidnap the girls Davis discovered the possibility that Moleski was recruiting young boys around Lloyd's age to lure little girls to Lloyd. Lloyd confessed to Davis the fact that he worried that the police would try to force him to confess to the kidnapping of girls.

Five hours had passed, Detectives decided hold a an informal meeting to examine the information Lloyd had provided them. It became difficult to decide if they should consider Lloyd as suspect or witness due to his inconsistent nature in the information he that he provided. But they did not overlook their suspicions that Lloyd requested immunity. If the immunity was granted to Lloyd however, the evidence he provided to police could be used against him. They also did not have any other suspects left alive, in the same way as Moleski and Helen Lloyd's girlfriend were deceased, so it was an extremely difficult decision to take. Davis and his colleagues reached an arrangement to

Lloyd, Davis told Lloyd that he was in talks with the prosecutor to look into his testimony.

After a couple of hours, detectives delivered a document to Lloyd's signature. The documents contained six bits of information that were in forms of an arrangement. The first was an agreement between Lloyd and Lloyd to only share accurate details about the incident. The second information also stated that Lloyd did not have any involvement in any crime. The third concern was to provide only reliable, truthful and accurate information provided by Lloyd in the hands of the police. The fourth aspect of the information was about any of his declarations not being utilized against the person who made them. The fifth agreement said that there was no immunity to be granted for any crime he committed against Sheila or Kate Lyon. The final agreement stipulated that no other terms were set forth against him.

Lloyd was unable to observe any contradictions in the agreement. The immunity offered to Lloyd included the fact the fact that he was participant in the crime, and if he confessed to being involved in the incident, the agreement was deemed null and void. Lloyd was able to sign the agreement. After he signed the document, Lloyd offered more details to the police. He claimed that he identified Moleski and acknowledged the fact that Moleski was the one wearing the jacket that contained the tape recorder the day the girls vanished, He also claimed that he observed the girls in the parking lot together with the man. Afterwards, they travelled to a vehicle with him. After witnessing Moleski and the kids, Lloyd began to become concerned, and made a report to the police. The new information was provided by him was portrayed as Moleski in the role of the kidnapper, and the police as witnesses. When asked about his knowledge about the disappearance of the girl and he claimed to have no of any knowledge however the story was reported on for several many days. Lloyd denied any involvement in the disappearance of the girl; after some hours of interrogation the man made comments that made detectives concerned about Lloyd. If asked what his view was on what happened the girls, he stated that there was a possibility that someone murdered, raped or burned the girl. After further questions, Lloyd said he admitted that he enticed the girls to go away by bringing in a tape recorder but that his family members were responsible for the raped and murder. He identified his brother Tedd, Dick his uncle and Lee his father.

In 2014, detectives started an extensive probe of the Welch family. They observed that the Welch family had had sexual experiences within the family. In the event that Lyon sisters were to have been with such people It was clear that the Welch family was aware of understanding of sexual offences committed by their Lyon sisters. Lloyd admitted that his uncle was the one who planned the kidnapping and the mass rape of the girls. Dick Welch was 70 years old when police rounded up his case for investigation. He was known for his violence towards family members. Dick maintained his responses to police in a consistent manner and they could see that he was not a nice person as well. In court in the year 2015 Dick Welch proclaimed his innocence, in contrast to Lloyd who was known to keep his inconsistent statements and claimed that he would assist the police to catch the culprit. Lloyd's brother Teddy was just 11 years old at the time of his abduction He also suffered two broken arms it is obvious that he would not be able to accomplish much. The other two cousins of Lloyd, Connie Parker, and Henry Parker admitted witnessing the burning of a duffle bag the fire; they also acknowledged that the bag was taken to the spot by Lloyd. Based on these investigations, police were able to determine the story of what Lloyd was like a few years ago.

As of 2015 Lloyd became a poor, shackled, and in need of help. In contrast to the teen Lloyd who was a rough and tough guy and always a snore of cigarettes and alcohol, Lloyd was always grungy and had long hair. When he was 18 Lloyd was now a predator and an armed criminal. He was free to roam and had done anything to make him feel happy. He was extremely attracted by women and would beat anyone he had relationships with. He recalled the Lyon sisters who were crying at the rear of the wagon. they were raped and dragged and then killed with an axe. Their bodies were chopped up to pieces, dismembered, and stuffed in a duffle bag that was green and tossed into a bonfire.

Detectives visited the location in which Lloyd claimed that his uncle had burned one of the bags. The pit was located under an archway near uncle Dick's home situated in Hyattsville, Maryland. Detective Davis visited Dicks home, but the house did not match Lloyd's description. Therefore, Davis drove nearby to Baltimore Avenue, where Lloyd's father Lee and his mother Edna resided. It was a duplex with two floors. The duplex was now in line with Lloyd's description. Lloyd had stated that Dick left the garage with two girls. Detective Davis was at the home in the afternoon the new owner was living there; Davis was talking with the tenant the tenant was the tenant was a Hispanic lady who could speak only a little English He had convinced her to investigate the basement, so then he began to search. He found the basement Lloyd had described in his account of his uncle Dicks home. The basement resembled an underground dungeon. Its ceiling was low and had poor lighting. It was also home to old furniture. The cellar appeared abandoned and he had a suspicion that something awful had happened there.

The next day, the forensics teams and investigators arrived on the scene. They were able take down the furniture and then spray the blue-star blood detection against the floor and walls. The agent bonds to tiny haemoglobin traces and emits a glowing glow when exposed to blue light. When the room was lit up they could see huge evidence of blood that looked as if somebody was slaughtered in the basement. The basement was closed from the outside; it was the exact basement that he told the police that he used to hang out and smoke pot when he was a child. The basement was also in which the girls were abducted, drugged, dismembered, and killed. When the detectives visited Taylor Mountain, the mountain which Lloyd claimed the bodies were burned in the bonfire, they saw an old cemetery without marked graves, and an enormous fire pit that was that was used to burn garbage The pit could burn for several days. The pit was designated as a crime scene , and was dug up. The police later talked to Dick Welch, but he did not seem to be able to provide any information about the girls who went missing. The discovery of the basement was a positive idea for detectives.

Additionally residents from Bedford County had made a grand jury statement about Lloyd Welch in 1975; they claimed that he was taken two duffle bags in the direction of Taylor Mountain; they also stated that they could smell that odor emanating from the flame that burned for a few days. Analyses couldn't identify any DNA in the blood that was found in the basement. However, it was evident that the blood came from human. Although Lloyd has denied that he killed the girls, he'd continue to spend the majority of his life in prison in 2017. In 2017 he was 60 years old and was sentenced to a minimum of 48 years in prison.

It's still a blessing that the majority of details of the girl's disappearance remain a mystery. There was also not any information about the people associated with Lloyd. Lloyd would say that he sought legal advice and that the request was not granted and he also claimed that he was required to appear before the detectives to be questioned, however, Lloyd seemed to be willing to divulge details during interrogation. There were other methods used by the detectives against Lloyd For instance, they made up stories about having evidence against Lloyd that was not true.

In his final interview with Lloyd in his final interview, he admitted that he was recruited by his uncle Dick to entice and choose the girls.

Lloyd claimed to be approximately 88 percent certain the girls were sexually assaulted and killed. The explanation he gave about leaving the girls with him after he offered pot to them made no sense. Mary and John were unable to imagine that their daughters would take pots from a complete stranger. They were six plus kids raised in the context of a Christian home. Another question that was intriguing was how an abductor could have seized charge of two young girls at the same time and the police began to believe that Helen was involved in helping Lloyd get the girls to leave because the latter was involved with prior criminal acts together with Lloyd. It was probable that they were held in the basement where blood was discovered. The detectives had to answer many hours and hundreds of interrogation to uncover a evidence of lies from Lloyd and finally putting it all together difficult. Lloyd lied throughout his interview and provided some information which helped in the investigation. A trained and skilled detective such as Davis could discern the truth behind the lies, with the aid of his interrogation techniques. The detectives discovered that worry of Lloyd being caught that brought him back to the mall in 1975, Lloyd actually thought that the mall could be a place to lie while at someone else. It is believed that for every conviction of a crime it is possible that there were various crimes committed by the same person. In 2017 the forensics team discovered a tooth at Taylors Mountain, and it was a 12-year-old The tooth was taken to the Bedford Sheriff's County, however, when it was time to be examined the tooth was discovered missing.

If one is to look at all the information and stories that were discovered in connection with this tale, and add in the fact that a human's teeth was discovered on the scene of the crime, and also certain beads that resembled those worn by the girls were found, one might draw a conclusion rather than an conclusive statement. The detectives were really determined and had removed a small portion of the cement that contained the blood out of the basement. Then they and then pulverized the material and then examined it. however, it was forty years ago, so any evidence of important information were erased. It was also evident that Lloyd was involved in the crime, however it was difficult to determine whether he was acting independently or with help. Lloyd was considered to be a monster , who eventually became an accomplice; he was victimized at the age of a child and grew up in a community of people who displayed such a cruel attitude. But, the police are proud of the work they had put into.

Chapter 5: The Messalina Of Ilford

January 9 September 1923

John Ellis had been England's Chief Executioner from 1907 onwards, and was a serious defender of his position. Contrary to many of his predecessors who weren't opposed to the practice of 'botching' an execution to show the public an entertaining spectacle in public executions, when they could be legalized, Ellis was focused on getting rid of executed criminals as fast and efficiently as was feasible.

In his professional life, he executed several of the country's most notorious killers, including the Dr. Hawley Harvey Crippen in 1910 and the poisoner Frederick Seddon in 1912, and Herbert Rowse Armstrong, the only UK solicitor ever to be executed for murder in 1922. Today, on this frigid winter day it was his turn at Holloway Prison to oversee the first woman's execution within England in the years since 1907.

Twenty-nine year old Edith Thompson had been sentenced to execution in December in connection with the death of her husband Percy. Her lover and suspected co-conspirator, Frederick Bywaters, was scheduled to be executed the next morning in Pentonville Prison less than a mile away. Bywaters would die to his death in silence, but the execution of Mrs. Thompson's death was set to cause the victims nightmares for many years to come.

When he walked into the cells, Ellis was greeted by a loud moan. Ellis spotted a petite and beautiful brunette lying on the floor, in an unconscious state. Two Warders (as prisoners were referred to during the UK) were seated over her, and spoke softly however, her only response was a series groans. Ellis recounted in his autobiography "She seemed dead, already."

In tandem together, the guards as well as Ellis two assistants helped lift Edith Thompson to her feet. The hangman then gently pinned her wristsand she taken across the narrow distance from the prison cell to the Gallows.

Because she was not able to stand, the guards held her up in the trap, while Ellis fitted straps to her thighs and ankles, and secured the noose to her neck. The lever was then pulled which was then Edith Thompson plunged to a quickly and mercifully swift death.

All that was left now was to prove that her sentence was executed. With the help of medical experts, Ellis went down the ladder and separated the curtains that were encircling the hanging body. The images he saw could have pushed him to eventually suicide.

Mrs. Thompson swayed silently, the tremors she felt were long were over. However, beneath the feet of her was a swollen the pool of blood. It was dripping across her legs, the flow being too dark and heavy for it to be menstrual in its origin.

There are many explanations as to the reason for the sudden discharge. One explanation was it was possible that she was pregnant at the time of her execution as well as miscarried. Or perhaps an earlier abortion caused uterine damage in such a way that the sudden loss of her body caused bleeding. There was no post-mortem performed to establish the reason, since the authorities wanted to ensure that the issue be forgotten as quickly as they could.

The doctors stared in stunned shock. John Ellis, who had completed more than 200 executions in 1923, stumbled out in the open in a state of shock, gasping and white "Oh Christ Oh Christ!"[8 His son later said that the execution of Edith Thompson was haunting him to the point of his passing.

Edith Jessie Thompson was known as a number of different names throughout her tragic and short life. To her family and friends she was Edie an enthusiastic and outgoing young lady with the ability to do business that she became the chief buyer for an British milliner. Her husband Percy was killed in the dark night of October and a series of carelessly written letters were discovered to link her to the murder and she was dubbed the 'Messalina from Ilford'. In the present, she is considered to be the victim of a system of justice that slammed successful and independent women to allow them to be hung for a crime that they didn't commit.

Edith Graydon was born on December 25, 1893, in Dalston which was a district of the working class located in the northeast region of London. The father of her, William, was a clerk at the Imperial Tobacco Company and her mother, Ethel, was a police officer's daughter.

From all accounts, it was an extremely joyful one. She was an avid dancer and displayed a unique acting talent, so maybe she envisioned a career performing on stage, just like other creative girls do. However, when she graduated from school, her ambitions for the stage were put aside to focus on an easier career path.

Edith was a brilliant maths teacher, and so she was quickly employed as a bookkeeper with Carlton & White's, a London milliner and importer of fabrics. Her attractive appearance and natural fashion, paired with good intellect, led to the eventual promotion to chief buyer of the business. She frequently traveled to Paris to look at new fabrics and provide purchasing suggestions.

Soon after graduating from school, 16-year-old Edith was introduced to Percy Thompson, who was three years older than her and was employed in a shipping company. The following year, they were engaged but she was young and career-focused to marry immediately. The engagement lasted for six years until the beginning of January 1915 when they finally got married. After that, they purchased an apartment in the fashionable Essex city of Ilford and began living a somewhat luxurious life.

In 1921, a nineteen-year-old vessel captain named Frederick Bywaters joined their social circle. Edith knew For more than nine years. He was referred to as 'Freddy'. She and her younger brother were school buddies. Then she was particularly aware of his appearance: Bywaters was handsome, active, and a bit sexy due to his numerous travels. Edith could not help but compare her husband in a negative way to his appearance: Percy

Thompson was staid and pragmatic, without any romantic inclination long gone.

"The circumstances surrounding the marriage were not ideal for happiness," Filson Young wrote in Notable British Trials. "Husband and wife made a livelihoods separately. They left the home at eight o'clock in the morning, and returned at 7 pm in the night. There were no kids, and so they had nothing in common other than the dorm life and it appears to have turned to a tense chapter of disputes, and the more serious problem that is the constant efforts of a husband to consider something as a right which should be given."[99

Bywaters joined Bywaters joined Thompsons as well Edith's sibling Avis for a long trip on The Isle of Wight in June 1921. The foursome had such enjoyable time that, when the vacation of the group ended, Percy Thompson invited the young steward to stay with them when the sea was not in use.

Edith could not have been happier. Edith and Bywaters began to get together shortly afterward. When Thompson discovered the affair in August, he took his wife's hand, slapped her multiple times, and then threw Bywaters across the floor before Bywaters could get in the way. The altercation among the men came to an end with Bywaters being removed from the home on August 5.

He had a hard time leaving, but he encouraged Edith to get divorced or at the very least divorce her husband. She resisted, saying she was worried about the scandal but in truth Edith Thompson didn't despise Percy enough to get rid of the relationship. She was financially stable and wasn't eager to compromise this. The gorgeous and young Bywaters fulfilled her desire for romance and sex, however, she didn't see a real possibility of a future with her brother's former friend.

When Bywaters was sent to England for a one-month assignment 9 September. The couple kept in touch. She addressed him as "Darlint" and signed every correspondence with the name Peidi. She waited for him when the time came to return in October, enjoying the romantic escape he embodied. Each time he took a trip away (there were two more trips prior to the month of October, 1922), Edith wrote frequently and welcomed him with a smile when he returned.

Her words offered Bywaters an impression of lying to her husband. In a letter from March 31 1922 she wrote:

Tonight I'm likely be going to die...not really...but don't put the mask on once more Darlint (sic) till the 26th of May. Doesn't it feel like many years away? To me, it does and I'll keep hoping and wishing every day that I'll never be required put on the mask later on . . . . This really is the last time you disappear like the way the way things are? We've said it before, darlint and I'm sure we did not succeed . . . But there won't be a success this time around darlint, and there shouldn't be, and I'm telling you. If you're doing the same time and again, I'll be to wherever you go. ....You'll never let me go and never again, unless the circumstances differ.

From left To Right: Freddy Bywaters, Percy Thompson, Edith Thompson (Author's Collection)

Edith also caused Bywaters into believing that she attempted to escape by murdering Percy. In a letter from the 30th of April, she stated she had crushed the glass light bulb that she then crushed and then mixed them into her husband's dish of mashed potatoes. In another instance, she admitted that she poisoned the food of her husband.

A lot of the adventures she recounted were similar to scenes from popular books. Freddy Bywaters would later say that he did not believe she was actually involved in anything like this. Edith Thompson had a flair for the dramatic and for her writing about a murder will numb the urge to do something about it. However, the letters were to be read out by jurors that did not have enough knowledge of her to know the distinction.

The enthralled teenager approached Percy Thompson and demanded that Thompson give Edith divorce. Thompson said, "I don't see how it is a problem for you."

"You are making Edie's life hell. You are aware that she isn't satisfied with your actions."

"Well I've acquired her and will take her in my home."

Bywaters realized that the sole way that he and the woman who he loved was to take Thompson from the photograph. It was by any means required.

The 3rd of October 1922 was a cool autumn day. In the evening Thompson and Edith Thompsons were at the Criterion Theatre in Piccadilly Circus to watch a show along with a couple called the Laxtons. Percy and Edith were not able to return to Ilford until after midnight. While walking on the dark, deserted Belgrade Road toward their Kensington Gardens home, they saw footsteps rushing towards their home from the back.

This was Bywaters. To Thompson the man yelled, "You have got to get rid of the woman you love."

"No!"

The young steward lunged. Later, he said that Thompson was preparing to grab an assault weapon, and Thompson pulled out the knife that he carried around. In the subsequent fight and he was stabbed by his adversaries numerous times. Following his arrest, he told police "The reason I took on Thompson was because he had did not behave like a man with his wife. I was unable to continue watching her behave as she did. I was not planning to kill , but rather to hurt him."

The people who lived in the area could hear Edith screaming and crying out, "No, don't!" After Thompson was unable to stand, Bywaters ran.

Dora Pittard, who was walking on Belgrave Road en route to her home in Endsleigh Gardens, was shocked to witness her mother Mrs. Thompson rush out of the darkness towards her.

"Oh my God can you please help me? My husband is sick and is bleeding!"

Miss Pittard and a man who was strolling around returned her to the spot the spot where Thompson was lying against the stone wall with blood dripping out of his mouth. They called a local doctor known as Maudsley who arrived to discover Thompson dead from multiple stab wounds , and Edith suffering from extreme anxiety.

She informed the doctors and police she was returning home from the Ilford station at the time that Thompson abruptly collapsed and gave grunting. The police surgeon removed the body in the morgue, and saw the severity of the knife's wounds, two officers from the Metropolitan Police's K Division went to the Thompson residence to ask the widow more.

Bywaters was also interviewed and questioned due to his resentment towards Percy Thompson was not secret. When Edith noticed her new lover in his station, she believed that he had confessed and she cried, "Why did he do this? He didn't deserve commit the crime. It's a fact. My husband was struggling to cope with Freddy Bywaters."

Bywaters was convicted of murder. A search through his bedroom discovered more than sixty letters written by Edith Thompson. It only took an instant glance at their contents to turn the widow's identity from being a victim to a suspect.

One was:

Sure, darlint you are jealous of him, but I want you to think that He is entitled by law to everything that you are entitled to love and nature. Darlint, you are jealous to the point that you'll commit a desperate act.

The letters provided the only genuine evidence linking Edith Thompson to her husband's death however, it was sufficient to bring her to justice and get her detained. British law stipulated that if two persons would like to kill a third and one of them commits the act on behalf of both, then both have the same guilt of killing.

At the beginning, Bywaters did not deny any information about the incident, but after being told of the fact that Ms. Thompson was being charged also, he was stunned.

"Why Mrs. Thompson? She wasn't aware of my actions."

The couple went to trial two months after on December 6, on the Old Bailey, which was London's courthouse for criminals. When Bywaters stood trial the prosecution presented him with excerpts from the letters which were referring to an unspecified plot or shared goal. If asked if the plot involved killing Edith's husband the defendant shook his head and claimed that Edith was talking about the possibility of a suicide pact. This was which was a prominent theme throughout the novels of romance she read. The idea was that If Thompson refused to grant her divorce the couple would be buried together, rather than be separated.

"She was astonished at the idea of expressing who she was," he said at one moment. "She would sit down to read the book and then imagine her self as the character from that book."

Bywaters confirmed the fact that Edith Thompson had been unaware of his plans for the night, and that his original goal was confronting her husband. If Thompson was reacted with a smug attitude, Bywaters saw red.

Her father, William Graydon, also maintained that some of the letters were just an invention of his daughter's imagination. A letter dated the 23rd of June, 1922, stated that Thompson had revealed Freddy and Edith's relationship to her father. When a portion of it was read out in courtrooms, Graydon was astonished.

"Thompson never approached me or made any complaint regarding my daughter's behavior by the name of Bywaters," he said. "That is pure imagination."

Edith's younger sister, Avis Graydon, was inquired about certain events she was believed to have played a role in. She shrugged in shock. "That is just the imagination of my sibling."

When Edith was called to give evidence and testify, she was an unprofessional witness. The self-pitying and melodramatic comments she made caused a negative impression on the jury and judge and her admission in denial about the facts surrounding her husband's death did not help.

"I was extremely angry, and I didn't want to speak out against Bywaters. Bywaters," she protested. "I was trying to protect him."

Filson Young who was present at the trial, didn't believe that she ever attempted to kill Percy Thompson. He wrote "It does not seem to be in keeping to her personality, the way I perceive it that, if she actually wanted to kill her husband she would have put the idea on paper and wrote reams of evidence. She would have committed the crime and then did (or wrote) absolutely nothing about the incident. A Borgia doesn't write but she does act."

The judge the judge, Mr. Justice Shearman, summed his case to jurors in a way that was fair in the areas of law were involved. When referring the case of Edith Thompson, he said, "You will not convict her unless you're convinced that she and she agreed that the man was to be executed when he ought to be killed, and that she knew that he would commit the crime, and she instructed him to do it and through an arrangement between them, he was doing it."

However, his dislike for the sexually sexy antics that both of the defendants engaged in was apparent. Shearman stated his wife. Thompson's writings as "full of the outpourings an absurd, but simultaneously, an unrepentant love."

On December 11, following an hour of deliberation, the jury came to a decision of guilty. The moment Justice Shearman pronounced the death sentence for both defendants Edith became hysterical, and Bywaters was loudly protesting her innocence.

In the course of trial the media as well as the general public were highly negative of the trial of both Bywaters and Thompson

However, after they were sentenced to be executed, public opinions abruptly changed. A lot of people believed that hanging women was an inhumane act while others admired Freddy Bywaters for his devotion to the woman whom he loved. A million people sign a petition asking William Bridgeman, the Home Secretary, to reduce death sentence to life prison.

Edith's family were allowed to meet her at her Old Bailey holding cell the night she was found guilty. She was still in a state of shock crying and screaming. As she saw her father she ran away from the police escorts she was in, grabbed him and cried, "Dad, take me home!"

Chapter 6: Let Him Have It"- The Tragedy Of Derek Bentley

"Let him take it!"

The phrase has immortalized in gangster films or crime thrillers. The gunfire never ceases the death of someone.

On the night of November 2nd 1952, the words caused the death of one London officers. A little over three months later the nineteen-year-old boy was executed for the words he spoke.

Derek Bentley hadn't pulled the trigger However, the prosecutor stated that he influenced the person who did by screaming, "Let him have it, Chris!" Now we have evidence to prove that he didn't do this.

******

Derek Bentley. (Author's Collection)

Derek Bentley was born on June 30th 1933. His early years were stricken by mental health issues. when a bomb exploded near his home within World War II, the building collapsed around him, leading to severe head injuries. The school he attended was not as exemplary and was arrested for the first time on March 28, 1948. He as well as another boy were accused of theft. In September 1948, he was sentenced to three years in Kingswood Approved School. Kingswood Approved School outside Bristol.

School officials conducted tests to determine the 15-year-old's mental age as 10-years-old. Another test revealed his IQ was just 66. Other test results were as bleak as An EEG reading showed that he had epilepsy and his reading abilities were similar to that of the five-year-old.

After the release of his father in June 1950 Bentley began to withdraw in his home, avoiding social engagement and cut ties with the handful of acquaintances he had. In 1952, at the time Bentley was just nineteen years old and was qualified for compulsory national service, doctors declared him mentally substandard as a result of which he was not fit for the military.

Encouraged by his family to find an employment opportunity, Bentley found employment at a furniture removal firm, however, he was then forced to quit due to a back injury in the year following. Once he had healed enough, he could move around without feeling pain, he was able to join his first job with the Croydon Corporation as a garbage collector, but his sluggish mobility and inattention time led him to be moved to street cleaning in just three short months. In September 1952, they dismissed him.

Depressed and angry, nineteen-year-old Bentley attempted to earn money using the only method that worked before. In the evening on November 2 1952, he teamed together alongside Christopher Craig, a sixteen-year-old fellow criminal. Their initial goal was to steal a butcher shop, but the store was so well-lit that they decided to leave. Unfazed, they decided to go after another goal that was their warehouse at Barlow & Parker, a confectionery manufacturer and wholesaler located in Croydon.

Both of them were arming themselves. Craig carried the Colt New Service .455 Eley calibre revolver that had its barrel removed by sawing so that it was easier to conceal. Bentley had a spiked, knuckleduster, as well as knives that his friend from high school had gifted him.

For the robbers who were planning to rob the girl who lived across the street was able to be watching out her bedroom window when she saw them leap across the gate to the warehouse. As they made their way through a drainpipe up and climbed up to the top, she called her father, who raced to the nearest telephone box and made a call to the police.

The moment a police unit was on the scene, Craig hissed, "It's a copper! You must hide behind us!"

He and Bentley were able to hide behind a roof shelter and waited. Within ten minutes, detective Sergeant Frederick Fairfax appeared and shouted, "I am a police officer! This area is secure!"

Inquiring about these two men Fairfax was able to get them over, and arrested Bentley. He then turned to Craig who had pulled his revolver from his pocket and declared, "Hand over the gun and let me know, young man."

Bentley was able to get free, and told his friend "Let him take it away, Chris! !'

Craig fired his gun and fired a bullet that grazed Fairfax's shoulder. Others police officers appeared and fired fire making the rooftop an area of war.

The Police Constable Sidney Miles hurried up the steps leading towards the rooftop. The veteran of 22 years with the Metropolitan Police Force had gotten keys to the building from the supervisor and was heading to Fairfax's help. When he went through the door on the roof and was struck by a bullet on the head immediately, killing him.

While Bentley could have taken out his knuckleduster, or knife, and easily defeated the wounded Fairfax, Bentley remained in the same spot. Craig however, in contrast, ran away after exhausted his ammunition. As more policemen came to his aid when he ran, he jumped off of the roof. The fall of 30 feet broke his left wrist and spine however he was able to recover.

Two of them were charged with murder for the killing of PC Miles. Derek Bentley's confession to police read like this:

I've been warned that I should not speak anything unless I choose to, however what I say is recorded in writing and possibly presented as evidence.

(signed) Derek Bentley

I've been friends with Craig since the time I was in school. We were rebuffed by our parents from going out with them, however we still went out together We have been out with each other until this evening. I was watching the television this evening (2nd

November , 1952) between 8pm and 9pm Craig came to me. My Mother opened the door after which I noticed her announce that I was gone. I had been earlier to see the pictures and came home around 7pm. A bit after, Norman Parsley and Frank Fazey called me. I didn't open the door nor did I speak to them.

My mother informed me that they called me and I fled to them. I walked and with them to the shop where I noticed Craig sitting. We sat and chatted, and the next thing I knew, Norman Parsley and Frank Fazey left. Chris Craig and I then caught a bus for Croydon. We departed on West Croydon and then walked across the road to which is where the toilets are located I believe it's Tamworth Road. When we got to the location where you saw Chris, Chris looked in the window. There was a small iron gate that was at the end of the. Chris then jumped me and followed. At that point, Chris was silent. We both walked up to the roof that was flat at the highest point. A gardener across the street hurriedly dangled at us with a torch. Chris declared: "It's a copper, you can hide here." We were able to hide behind a shelter setup on the rooftop. We waited for about 10 minutes. I didn't know that he would make use of the gun. A simple-clothed man was able to climb up the drainpipe, and then onto the roof. The man declared: "I am a police officer and the area is completely surrounded." He grabbed me (and) when we were walking out of the building, Chris fired. There was no one else around at the moment. We went with the policeman around a corner and came across the door. The door opened and a cop wearing a uniform appeared. Chris fired again and the policeman fell to the ground. I could tell the injuries he sustained since a large amount of blood gushed out from his forehead, just over his nose.

The policeman pulled him around the corner in front of the brickwork entryway to the front door. I can remember shouting something, but I'm not sure the exact wording. I couldn't see Chris as I yelled at him. He was behind an invisible wall. I heard policemen outside the door. the officer with me stated, "I don't think he has any more bullets." Chris said "Oh yes, I've got" and fired again. I believe I saw him fire three times in total. The policeman then shoved me down the stairs , and I could not see other. I was aware that we were planning to enter the building but I didn't know the kind of things we'd take - but just what could be taken. I didn't have an arsenal and didn't know Chris owned one until he fired. I'm now aware that the policeman wearing a uniform has died. I ought to have mentioned that after the plain-clothed policeman went to the drainpipe to arrest me, a second policeman wearing uniform walked in when I heard somebody calling Mac.. He was in the same room as us when the other officer was killed.

This statement was given to me and it is true.

(signed) Derk [sic] Derek W. Bentley

Statement I made and transcribed by the Det Sgt Shepherd who read it over, and signed from J. Smith DI.

The murder trial started with the Old Bailey on December 9 the 9th of December, 1952. The public was in a frenzy against the defendants since the prevalent belief of 1952 was that young groups were infiltrating London and killing those who attempted in their way to stop them. In the year prior the year before, four police officers were killed while on duties, and people complained that someone should be paid for the murder of PC Miles.

Each of Craig and Bentley have pleaded guilty in front of Lord Goddard Lord Goddard, the Chief Judge of Lord Goddard. While Derek Bentley had not fired the fatal bullet or was able to resist arrest The trial against him was based around one major issue.

British law states that when more than two persons are involved in the same crime, they may be equally accountable where there is evidence of a common motive. The now famous phrase "Let him take Chris! Chris!" were used to prove that two youngsters planned to murder the police officer.

The defense argued that Bentley has never made the claim. (The authorities were the only one to claim that he made such a statement.) The lawyer for the defendant, who was 19 years old, stated that, even if he did the gun, he could likely to have said, "Give him the gun."

Uncertainty arose over the amount of shots fired, as well as the shooter. The bullet that claimed the life of PC Miles was never found or identified, and a ballistics specialist said that the sawed off barrel on Craig's gun might be a factor in the ability of his gun to hit an object within a specific distance. The lawyer for the teenager emphasized to jurors that the veteran police officer could equally easily been killed through friendly shooting.

Derek Bentley's capability to stand trial was initially questioned. A psychiatrist from Maudsley Hospital stated that the young man was unliterate and borderline retarded. However the Chief Medical Officer (head of the nation's medical services) admitted that, while Bentley's intellect was not high however, he wasn't considered to be a "feeble-minded" person under the Mental

Deficiency Act. While Scottish law acknowledged the notion impaired mental capacity, English legislation did not yet, and it would not be until the passing in the Homicide Act of 1957. The only valid medical defense to a murder case was criminal insanity. Bentley was not insane.

Lord Goddard was adamant about the reality that Bentley was Armed with a knife as well as a the knuckleduster (even even though Craig provided the pair of weapons) and had voluntarily gone to the warehouse in order to commit a crime that could be violent. The summary he provided clarified that he was convinced of their guilt.

In one instance Goddard declared, "Hey, "...see what Bentley was wearing on his body. What's the knife?" When it was handed to him , he put it on, before proceeding:

It was apparently given to Bentley by Craig the knuckleduster was not his own, however Bentley was armed with the knife. Do you remember seeing such a horrifying weapon? It's designed to punch someone directly in the face by a person who is threatening you. It is grasped here and your fingers slide through--I can't quite make it through, but I'm sure it's there--and you've got yourself a terrifyingly steel bar that you can strike anyone with. You can kill someone with thisbar, no doubt. Have you ever seen something more terrifying than this? There's an iron spike that can punch anyone that comes up to you; in case the blow from the steel isn't sufficient to be enough, you've an additional spike on the edge to strike. It is yours to test, if you would like, while you go back to the room. It's a shocking weapon. This is Craig Armed with the revolver and sheath knife. Bring me that sheath knife. It's the large one. One has to wonder what the parents are thinking today and allowing a young man who is 16 -- they say they aren't sure however, why wouldn't they know?--to own a knife like this , which he can carry on the go? This isn't a brand new weapon, as you observe; it's well-worn. This is what Craig was discussing. What's that other knife? Here's Bentley with an a little smaller knife, yet you can feel that it's sharp and sharp. What does he carry inside his coat, and not with a sheath? [12]

The jury took only 75 minutes to decide Christopher Craig and Derek Bentley guilty of murder. Since he was not yet 18 years old, Craig was sentenced to be held in prison "at the discretion of Her Majesty's Court" while the 19-year-old Bentley was sentenced to death.

While the jury suggested mercy in Bentley's case However, the Lord Goddard did not mention the same thing in his post-trial reports to the Home Office. In August 1970 , he advised the writer David Yallop that he thought Bentley would be released and his opinion was irrelevant.

The mistake proved fatal for the condemned teenager. It was the Court of Appeal dismissed Bentley's petition on the 13th of January 1953 and concluded that if the trial judge had no reason to suggest an appeal the court had no basis to interfere .

Derek Bentley's fate lay in the control by the home secretary Sir David Maxwell Fife.

******

William Bentley, Derek's father was the man who created a public awareness campaign that helped bring sympathy to Derek's son. People who supported Bentley argued that his impaired mental health and low intelligence made him a perfect imitation of the smart and imposing Craig. He was carrying weapons that were deadly due to the fact that his friend's younger son had handed them over to him initially.

Fife eventually refused to give the relief. Bentley's friends and family figured they knew that Home Secretary was looking for someone to cover the cost of the murder of the police constable and also act as a deterrent for future criminals. Because Craig was not able to be a candidate for death sentence, Derek Bentley drew the short straw.

The public was shocked by the injustice , and even Parliament was involved by having more than 200 MPs signing petitions urging for the Home Secretary's reconsideration. The petition read:

We, the members undersigned of the Commons House of Parliament, considering the advice offered by you to Her Majesty the Queen in relation to the matter of Derek Bentley to be grievously incorrect and not in accordance with the normal legality of the matter We respectfully request that you recommend to her Majesty the Queen to apply the royal right to mercy, so that the death sentence upon him is not carried out.

William Bentley, accompanied by Christopher Craig's mother, visited the Home Office to beg the Secretary of State to reconsider his decision, but a representative told the father who was devastated of the fact that his decision would be made final.

The crowds gathered at Whitehall and the House of Commons and Whitehall protested, shouting "Bentley should not die" and "Bentley deserves to be granted reprieve". As police blocked from the Home Office entrance, the demonstrators were not dissuaded; they continued to the home of Sir David Maxwell-Fyfe and then to Downing Street. They continued to demonstrate until shortly after 22:00 a.m. They fought police every time their protests were stopped.

The day of the hanging, the 28th of January, a large crowd gathered in front of Wandsworth Prison. According to all reports, Derek Bentley went quietly to the grave and his hangman Albert Pierpont, did an impeccable job. However, if the Lord Goddard and the Home Secretary, or anyone else who was in support of the execution believed that Derek Bentley would not be remembered They were totally wrong...

www.ingramcontent.com/pod-product-compliance
Lightning Source LLC
Chambersburg PA
CBHW060332030426
42336CB00011B/1302